50 YEARS OF
FLYING
THRILLS AND CHILLS

GORDON L LEVIN, MD

Copyright Registration Number: 1-15032234721

Published by

www.owlpublishers.com

360 S Market St, San Jose, CA 95113, United States.

Printed in the United States of America

DEDICATION

This book is dedicated
to my loving wife, Judy Levin, and co-adventurer.
Thank you for walking beside me through every chapter of
this journey.
And to David Ganz, my inspiration and mentor, whose
guidance continues to light my path.

CONTENTS

Chapter 1: US Navy.. 1

Chapter 2: Instrument License 20

Chapter 3: Civilian Life Flying San Jose...................... 23

Chapter 4: Winter Flying 47

Chapter 5: Alaska 55

Chapter 6: Africa 82

Chapter 7: Cross Country 90

Chapter 8: Mexico 98

Chapter 9: Charity Flights.. 110

Chapter 10: Emergencies and Risky Flying............... 116

Chapter 11: There are Old Pilots and Bold Pilots, But No Old, Bold Pilots.
.... 129

About the Author 133

INTRODUCTION

Flying became one of my hobbies, and after 50 years, as this came to an end, I realized I had an extensive experience that few pilots have enjoyed. I took out my logbooks and recalled my trips, actually reliving them, bringing back memories of both the thrills and the scary times. For some reason, there seemed to be plenty of excitement, both good and marginal, that few pilots can (or maybe will) talk about.

The flying stories in this book are true, though at times I have combined one or two trips into a single account to keep the flow engaging. The emergencies described are real, as are the flights, though they rely in part on memory. I have tried to specify which plane I was flying, since the book is arranged by chapters rather than by strict chronology

Born and raised in the Washington, D.C. area, I grew up in a simple, middle-class neighborhood, attended public schools, and graduated from the state university. I worked my ass off putting myself through college and medical school, though in the state of Maryland, the tuition for college was $90 a semester and medical school $500 a year. This was the 1960s, and I feel I was fortunate to have grown up in that era and in a state that catered to students.

To be honest, life was somewhat boring. I didn't excel at anything but just plodded along in my middle-class environment, until I entered the U.S. Navy!!

This story is, in essence, my experience since that time and how the Navy changed my life. During those years, I progressed up the aeronautical ladder, obtaining my commercial license and then my Airline Transport License, or ATP. I figured that would count toward lowering my insurance, though I am not sure it did. With all that, I guess I felt invincible, and in the stories that follow, I seemed to fly that way. To be sure, I was lucky enough to get through situations where the odds were probably against me. This is a summary of my flight experiences.

CHAPTER 1: US NAVY

I first became enamored with flying when my sister started dating a student Marine pilot. He was stationed in Pensacola, FL, and we lived in Silver Spring, MD. While he was dating my sister, he would commute using space-available military air from Pensacola to Andrews Air Force Base in Washington, DC. The good news was that it was free; the hitch was that there was no real schedule to count on.

When he was lucky enough, after waiting to see if a plane would head north to Maryland, he could fly as a passenger. He would usually stay with me in my bedroom at home from Friday night until he had to get back to Pensacola by Monday morning. We would drive him back to Andrews Air Force Base on Sunday morning, hoping there were flights south as he tried to get a free military flight.

This was always risky, as there were no scheduled or guaranteed flights. These flights were at the whim of what was needed to fly between Washington, DC, and Pensacola, FL. If, for some reason, he couldn't get back to base by Monday morning, he would have to sit at the end of the runway in Pensacola, making sure all student pilots had their wheels down for landing.

For me, this was thrilling, not being sure of anything except possibly a weekend with my sister, taking calculated risks. While he stayed with us, he would tell me about the training he was getting and the wonderful experiences of going through the military flight training program, similar to those I also experienced, which will be described further in the book. As an impressionable 13-year-old boy, this sounded wonderful and, of course, planted the germ of flying in my brain.

When I was in medical school at the University of Maryland in 1964, I knew I was going to have to go into the military. The Vietnam War was raging. Even with the school deferment came the obligation as a physician; there was no way of getting out of military or government service, no matter what number I had. Since the Air Force had bases in Montana and the Army had bases in Texas, it was an easy decision to choose the Navy, with bases in San Diego, San Francisco, as well as the big cities on the East Coast.

I also found out that they had a summer job opportunity for medical students. One of the job opportunities was in Pensacola, FL, which of course stimulated the little germ of flight training glorified by the young Marine flight student, who by this time had become my brother-in-law, David Ganz. I opted for the summer externship offered to physicians as an Ensign in the U.S. Navy.

There is no better place to get indoctrinated into U.S. Naval and Marine flight operations than Pensacola Naval Air Station. While there, I learned about another program for medical students: six months of training to become a Flight Surgeon. These six months of training were not counted as part of the obligated 24 months as a doctor. The training included four months of aerospace medicine and two months of actual flight training. I was hooked.

After my internship at Highland General Hospital, Oakland, CA, I signed up for an extra six months of my military obligation to become a Flight Surgeon.

On July 1st, I reported to Pensacola U.S. Naval Air Base, put on my bronze railroad tracks on my shoulders as a Lieutenant, and started the program for Flight Surgeon. The classroom courses included subjects important to the health of a pilot and potential astronaut, which covered cardiology, pulmonology, ophthalmology, and psychology. The Navy certainly wanted its pilots to be able to see well, not have a possible lingering heart attack or breathing problem, and to be mentally stable.

At the time, in the 1960s, the government invested about $500,000 in training pilots, and they wanted to make sure that they were the healthiest candidates with the least chance of any medical or psychological breakdowns. That was the whole idea of the Flight Surgeon program: to reduce the chances of losing these men as pilots.

The other part of the training program for the Flight Surgeons was to understand the stresses of flying, and the best way was to place the Flight Surgeon in a plane as a pilot to at least understand the basics of flying. The Air Force never trained their Flight Surgeons. For two months, Flight Surgeon training included flying the T-28 trainer with 1,425 horsepower. This was actually the second plane, the regular potential pilots would upgrade to from a smaller trainer, the T-34 with only 225 horsepower.

While I was going through the Flight Surgeon program, I decided to take private flying lessons during the first four months, which were mostly academics. Looking back at my first logbook, my first private flight lesson was in a Piper PA-28-140 on July 26, 1969, in Pensacola, Florida. After 7.7 hours of instruction, I first soloed on August 14, 1969, and passed my private pilot flight test on December 17, 1969, after 44.6 hours of instruction. I guess things were simpler back in those days, since I understand most student pilots now need about 60 hours of flight training to be signed off as private pilots.

This was the first time in the past four years that I actually had some time to take flight training; prior to that, it had been school, with all non-classroom time devoted to studying or hours on the hospital wards. Even then, with my fresh pilot's ticket, I barely flew, having been transferred to Camp Pendleton and awaiting my assignment to the First Marine Base in Danang, Vietnam

During this period, when the military flight training started, I switched between the Piper, with 140 horsepower, and the 1,500-horsepower T-28. The flight characteristics were markedly different. As Flight Surgeons, we were allowed to solo the T-28. To say that it was a monster of a plane in which to learn the basics is an understatement.

An episode involving one of the other students brought this home. While he was on the left landing pattern in the T-28, a gust of wind put the left wing in a precariously low position.

4

Realizing his predicament, his first instinct was to add full power, and the torque from the engine rolled him back to a normal position. He hadn't even thought of using his rudder to realign the plane. Had he been on the right base, the extra power would have completely inverted the plane, with the torque of the engine leading to a disastrous result.

Boarding T28 for flight training as flight surgeon

As Flight Surgeons, we were put through most of the emergency training that the designated aviators (future military pilots) went through. This included the Dilbert Dunker. This device was engineered to simulate the possibility of ditching a plane in the ocean. It consisted of a simulated cockpit on a rail that would travel 10 feet into the depths of a swimming pool, invert, and then sink to the bottom. The idea was to learn how to escape from an inverted plane in the water. Good training, but pretty scary. Wondering if I would get caught underwater and need oxygen from the scuba divers. I love to swim, but the thought of drowning is a real downer.

My brother-in-law described his first encounter with this trainer. The applicant before him had borrowed some tennis shoes that were too big. When the dunker hit the water and inverted, his feet were pushed forward, and the extra length of the shoes got stuck under something. It took the Navy divers, who were in the water for such emergencies, to give him oxygen since they couldn't extricate him from the cockpit. The Dilbert Dunker was put in reverse, and he came back to the surface alive, slung over the front of the cockpit, a bit shaken to say the least. The instructor told him to get back in line to redo the training, then turned to my brother-in-law and said, "Next."

We also underwent simulated ejection seats. This was a pretty simple device: a chair mounted on a rail that was almost vertical, up to about 25 feet. As I sat there waiting, having no real idea what the experience would be and anticipating a painful slap in the buttock, there was a loud bang, and I was shot up like out of a cannon to the top of that rail. The blast they used was about two-thirds of the normal ejection seat, but you got the idea, and if you needed it, you'd certainly use it. I never wanted to leave a perfectly flying plane, but I had great confidence knowing the ejection seats were there when they were needed. I almost had a chance to experience that part of the plane, but I'll save that for later.

Another experience we were put through was to be dragged behind a PT boat tethered to a parachute harness. This was to simulate landing in the water while still connected to the parachute and being dragged around by the wind at 40 miles an hour. It may seem a simple matter to release a parachute and unhook the connections, simple on land, but this was known to be the cause of many deaths among pilots, especially during the previous wars.

Dropped from PT boat with parachute harness with training to unleash from speeding PT boat

The platform was rigged on the upper superstructure of the PT boat, simulating a pirate's plank, high above the waterline. I stood out on the plank, strapped into the simulated parachute with my helmet on. It was scary to be standing on the outcropping of a plank, on a boat going 40 mph, about to be knocked off, falling 30 or 40 feet into the water, and then dragged at about 40 miles an hour. The idea was to unhook the straps that held the parachute lines and not panic. The interesting part was that when I was standing on dry ground, the release of the parachute was right at shoulder level. But when you were being dragged, it was much higher, and you had to realize where it was in that position. Funny, no one told us about that discrepancy.

Standing on the plank, having watched the candidates before me and thinking about what was about to happen, the metal rig holding the parachute lines dropped, hitting me on the top of my helmet and knocking me off the plank: splash and realization. I was dragged like a fish on a line. Before I found the hinges, I swallowed a lot of water as I grabbed at my shoulders. Finally, panic receded, thinking returned, and I realized the release latches were much higher.

We also had training in the high-altitude chamber to experience hypoxia. Sitting in the pressure chamber, about a half dozen of us lined up on the benches, the chamber was synthetically elevated by reducing the pressure. This decreased the oxygen available to breathe compared to sea level. We were all wearing oxygen masks, and at altitude, we were told to remove them. Hypoxia isn't particularly painful, but it isn't long before you just can't think very well. The point of the training was clear, especially when we tried to play patty cake with one another. All coordination was gone, and pat-a-cake quickly turned into hitting your partner's face with slapping hands.

Another experience we endured was the spinning chair to simulate vertigo. This played games with the semicircular canals in the inner ear. It wasn't fun, but it showed how head movement while in a spin would disorient you. This demonstrated the feeling of the "leans," thinking you weren't sitting straight when you were actually leaning. This is a very common situation while flying when you can't see the horizon. Flying in the clouds without a proper training (instrument license) is a very common cause of crashes for the uninitiated.

At the completion of our six-month training program, we had options on where we would like to be stationed. My choice was with the First Marine Air Wing in Vietnam. I wasn't the only one wanting this assignment; about one-third chose Vietnam. I guess we all wanted some adventure, and at that time, we were also pretty gung-ho about the war in Vietnam. We were clearly naïve and very young. Other choices included aircraft carriers, land-based hospitals, and flying with the Blue Angels, the premier assignment, especially for single physicians. The caveat, however, was that if the Flight Surgeon who was to go to Antarctica for a year was unable to do so, the Blue Angel Flight Surgeon would take his place. That is exactly what occurred.

I was stationed at the Danang air base, which was a combination of the Air Force on the south side and the Marine Air Wing on the north side. I was the Flight Surgeon for several units: VMFA 225, an A-6 Intruder squadron, and VMFA 232, an F-4 Phantom jet squadron. I was able to fly in the navigator seat or the RIO (radar interceptor officer) seat, not only on weekend practice/training (pleasure) flights around Japan and Korea, for the pilots to keep their skills, but also on combat flights in South Vietnam. The navigators and RIOs were happy to give up the time in the plane during these combat missions.

One flight in the Phantom jet was particularly exciting. As I was in the tandem seat, which has relatively small triangular side windows, the pilot suggested we give some excitement to the radar operators who were stationed on a hill just protruding over the Pacific. I wasn't sure what he meant, but so what? I had full confidence in the pilot. We lowered to 50 feet above the water, increased speed to .9 Mach, about 400 mph, made three aileron rolls, and then he yanked the stick to put us up into a vertical, straight skyward climb to 20 thousand feet to a hammerhead stall. In the back seat, looking out the windows, all I could see was the water and sky switching back and forth as the plane rolled, and then the G forces as we climbed. I had no choice in this maneuver, but I was thrilled to have enjoyed the experience. During the event, however, my mind raced to the times the student pilots would show off to their girlfriends over the beaches of Pensacola, not quite getting the maneuver correct, and auguring into the beach. Flying with the Marines, I learned there are no better pilots. If you are willing to land a jet on a moving carrier, at night, in a stormy sea, you have to have skill and guts. I have all the respect for these pilots and have never doubted them.

Phantom F4 fighter wingman over Mt. Fugi, Japan. Photo by G. Levin

Another time, while flying around Japan in the F4 on a fun trip to an Air Force base with a wingman in another F4 Phantom jet, I was physically forced up to the canopy as the plane took a sudden plunge earthward. All I actually saw was the wingman, whose plane seemed to deviate upward. Knowing the Marine pilots liked to play games, I thought it would be a good idea to know what was going on. To communicate with the pilot, I had to pull myself back, with some effort, into the seat so my foot could reach the intercom button on the floor. Finally, I got my answer. The vertical-horizontal stabilization system had failed, and he was trying to get the plane under control with the stick. We were proposing through the sky. I was getting ready to eject and was actually looking forward to a controlled ejection, though explaining it to the Admiral would be a downer. Not my problem, but the pilot would be dancing on the carpet. I figured we'd go over the water to prevent any damage to the property or population below. With a sinking stomach, I was trying to remember if I had pre-flighted the ejection seat. I usually did, but I just couldn't specifically recall. There wasn't anything I could do about that now. I envision in my mind the act of conducting safety checks.

It was decided to make it to an Air Force airport, though the plane was still jerking up and down. The pilot was getting better with practice, but still not 100 percent under control. As we arrived at the Air Force airport just south of Tokyo, I noticed a lot of cars pulled off the road with people outside looking at our plane like it was about to crash. Just on the final, the pilot lost the airspeed indicator and the plane sharply nosed down. He pulled it up, gunned it, and we went for a missed approach. Well, I tell you, the Marine pilots are the best! That's when he told me and his wingman we needed to fly off the wing of the second F4 as a speed indicator. Just an extra complication on a tricky landing. The second attempt was successful. Too bad for all the spectators. As I said, I had full confidence in the Marine pilots. I also had full confidence in the ejection seats.

While stationed at Danang Air Base, I was able to fly combat missions as well. I flew with the A6 Intruder on close air support of our troops when they were pinned down by enemy fire. In the A6 Intruder, there were side-by-side seats, which were much more comfortable as vision straight ahead was uncompromised. Since close air support was done visually, I didn't need to know how to operate the computer the navigator used for precision bombing; all I had to do was count the thousands of feet as we sped down to 2000 feet in elevation, going about 350 mph before pulling up. That's not much space while making a U-turn upward in the air at 350 mph.

A6 Intruders for close air support in flight formation. Photo by G.Levin

The first time out, I wasn't sure what to expect. We were directed to the drop zone by the forward air controller at about 10,000 feet and at what compass direction for the descent. I was to call out our altitude as we zoomed earthward. I was calling out the descending thousands quite rapidly, knowing that we were to drop the bombs at 2000 feet and pull up to get away. True to the Marines' need to get the bombs dropped accurately, he chose a lower altitude. As we got closer to 1000 feet, he said, "Release the bombs." Again, I had to wonder what was happening, knowing we should have pulled up at 2000 feet. Just after release, we pulled up to get away. My G suit inflated to prevent me from passing out from the 6 G forces, and the A6 inverted. Now, that's an unexpected sensation one doesn't experience often! I thought we were hit by small-arms fire, but it was just the pilot inverting to get a better view of where the bombs landed. I just loved flying with the Marines!

I had opportunities to fly in other aircraft. On one mission, I flew in the back seat of an OV-10. This is a relatively small twin-engine plane with guns, no bombs. Our mission of two OV-10s was to find the Viet Cong hidden in the trees or bushes. I was advised by the pilot before takeoff, and I took my flak jacket off and sat on it for the flight. One plane would fly at treetop level, and the other would fly 2000 feet higher. The idea was for the lower plane to draw fire from below, and when it did, the higher plane would swoop down with the firepower. I guess I was just bait. My pilot got the short straw. There was no action that day. Flying in the back seat of a plane, maneuvering in high humidity and temperature, wasn't a picnic, especially waiting for someone to shoot the plane down. Luckily, I don't get airsick, but it wasn't the best conditions.

I also had opportunities to fly in various helicopters. On one occasion, I was given the opportunity to fly the Cobra. The Cobra had tandem seating with the gunner sitting in front of the pilot, but the gunner also had a stick to control the Cobra, perhaps if the pilot behind was incapacitated. I got an appreciation of flying the helicopter when the pilot put it in a hovering position and gave me a chance to keep it there. It didn't take very long for us to start oscillating back and forth. It took practice to learn how to hover, and I don't think everybody is able to do that easily.

Viet Nam OV 10 wingman with rockets searching for viet Cong.
Photo by G. Levin

My experience in the Hueys on the medevac flights was in the cabin and not up front with the pilots. As a Flight Surgeon, there's not much you can do other than splint, start IVs, apply pressure, or give morphine. Usually, the corpsmen are on these flights, and I must hand it to them; it's a stressful and trying job. Using a stethoscope is impossible; the noise and the vibrations prevent any hope of hearing. The best thing about these helicopters is getting the wounded back to the triage center. I can't tell you how impressed I was with the medical triage system that was set up.

The wounded were brought in from the helicopter with their stretchers placed on sawhorses. Corpsmen on either side stripped them as a trauma physician, positioned between two stretchers, and examined the wounded. The chief surgeon would get a report of wounds and expectations from the examining physicians and decide who would go to the operating room first and who would be placed in the section for "expectation" and made comfortable. These physicians were specialists. I had just completed an internship and was nowhere near qualified at this point in the care of these mass casualties.

While in Danang, I was sent to the Philippines for a several-day course in escape and evasion. The flight was in an Air Force C-121 with about 30 troops and several civilians. I was seated next to a very attractive civilian woman. After we were in cruise mode, the pilot came out and asked me if I wanted to sit in the copilot seat. I guess he saw my Flight Surgeon Wings. The obvious reason was for him to sit next to his girlfriend, not that he needed a rest. Obviously, I loved the chance to sit in the cockpit. As the plane flew on using autopilot, I asked the right-seat copilot if we could disengage the autopilot and let me hand-fly the twin-engine C121. I was in my glory, hand-flying the plane, and after about 10 minutes, the pilot from my previous seat came into the cockpit. He then asked if I'd put the autopilot back on as he pulled the curtain back so I could see the occupants in the back of the plane: the last four rows had everyone barfing into the little paper bags. I got the idea that my straight and level hand-flying wasn't straight and level as I thought. A good lesson.

Returning to the States after my Vietnam stint, my actual

flying took a steep decline. Most of my time was spent in the Oak Knoll Naval Hospital as an orthopedic surgeon resident. Coincidentally, many of the patients I treated were the war wounded of Vietnam, and they made for very interesting learning cases. I still received flight pay even if I accumulated flight hours as a passenger, so I would find flights out of Alameda Air Base in Learjets while on training missions. I just sat in the back studying my medical books, occasionally checking the position of the plane in the sky.

I did not operate an aircraft until October 1975, when I was assigned to Jacksonville Naval Hospital. At that time, I flew from Craig Field to update my pilot's license and complete the biennial flight review. It was great just to get in the left seat and control the Piper. The thrill of flying and again feeling the wheels lift off the concrete, as if I had the wings and not the plane. The time in Jacksonville was like being in Wonderland. I had worked hard all my life: construction work while in high school and college, studying hard to get into medical school, and later, while in my residency, with little time for much else. But here I was, renting a house on the shore of the St. Augustine River with my wife-to-be, Judy, who came with me from San Francisco, and into a job as an orthopedic surgeon in a military hospital, a non-pressure practice, and starting to fly again.

The rental house had a dock on the St John's where I could dock my 20' sailboat, and the owner of the rental sold me his motorboat. What more could I ask for?

There, I met a pilot who, at the time, was looking for partners in a Lake Amphibious seaplane. The idea was to buy a new Lake, get our seaplane ratings, and sell new ones. It sounded like a great idea: get a new rating and make a little money on sales. Well, it was good in that it was fun to get the seaplane rating, but financially, the plan ended there. We never sold a plane. Once, I flew the plane to New Orleans, where they had a seaplane ramp on Lake Pontchartrain. In flying west from Pensacola VFR, all I had to do was fly over Interstate 10. The cruise speed on the Lake was about 80 mph. I found myself following a truck on Interstate 10 that seemed like I couldn't pass. Frustrating! The headwinds slowed the plane even more. I finally was able to pass the truck only by cutting the corner on the interstate's long curve. A good lesson for the future for buying a plane with more power.

One weekend, I flew with several buddies to Bermuda in the Lake. We stopped in Palm Beach, refueled, and headed to the island airport, Marsh Harbor. The weather started to close in, and since I didn't have my instrument license yet, I flew lower as the ceiling dropped to maintain VFR. Unfortunately, as I approached the island with the airfield, I was so low I couldn't find it. I could barely even find the island. Not to worry, we were in a seaplane, and if worst came to worst, we could land in the water. As I looked at the sea below, the waves looked a bit high for a nice water landing. All the water landings I had ever done were on the river, where the waves rarely maxed at a single foot. Now I was getting worried and trying to decide on which alternative I could take if I couldn't find the airport. After circling around for about 15 minutes, we finally spotted the runway through the murk of low clouds and landed. I truly appreciate GPS, which has since become commonplace, but it was still 3 years off.

CHAPTER 2: INSTRUMENT LICENSE

When you first lift the wheels off the ground, the sensation is unforgettable. Every new step in flying, each maneuver, each challenge brings its own thrill. With time, flying becomes more than discovery. It becomes a skill to refine, a freedom to enjoy. Yet the skies can also teach disappointment. You make plans, only to watch them unravel when the weather closes in. That frustration is often what pushes a pilot to pursue an instrument license. It is the key to real freedom: the ability to fly when you want to, where you want to, and not just when the skies allow. While stationed in Jacksonville, I took advantage of the GI Bill and started my instrument licensing training at St. Augustine. You cannot beat the military GI Bill. I finally earned my license to fly in the clouds, a great improvement in safety and the ability to actually go when you want to go, weather notwithstanding. Of course, there is weather and there is weather. One must distinguish between the two, which can be tricky, as you will learn from my tales.

Two factors influenced my decision to pursue an instrument rating: the relevant experience described above and the GI Bill, which covered 90 percent of the costs for commercial and instrument licenses. During my time in Jacksonville, I traveled to St. Augustine Airport to begin instrument training. The initial lesson took place in a Piper PA-151 on June 6, 1976, and I received my instrument certification on June 11, 1977.

To pilots who started flying in the latter 20th century,

instrument flying was a lot more challenging. Let us start with the simple basics of communication. Headphones and head-mounted microphones were virtually unavailable. The overhead audio speaker frequently produced static, requiring the user to hold the microphone close to their mouth with one hand. This often left only one hand free to operate the steering wheel, navigate using charts, switch frequency channels, record new headings, and make altitude adjustments. Remember, GPS technology had not yet been invented or was not yet accessible in general aviation aircraft.

The FBO (Fixed Base Operator) was established to help veterans obtain their commercial and instrument ratings. It took a minimum of 200 hours of dual instruction. In an hour of such instruction, the pressure was constant with the instructor sitting beside me, critiquing every mistake and occasionally offering praise. Unlike the seaplane rating, this was by far the most intense rating to obtain. The rules and regulations were extensive, and every lesson was drilled in. The flying part was not enjoyable until you actually completed the approach or maneuver properly. I was ecstatic when I landed these approaches successfully, and it became easier to continue the grinding training regimen. With more instruction, these positive reinforcements made it a little easier to come back for the next lesson. While driving down from Jacksonville to St. Augustine, I would imagine actually flying the car on instruments.

Since I was already into flying, I convinced Judy, my new wife, to take flying lessons. I figured, as she did, that having some idea of flying would make her more comfortable, especially if she had to take the controls in an emergency. She bought a guaranteed solo flight course at a public TV auction for a mere $150, and eventually soloed. Though she never really felt comfortable being alone in the sky, she was more confident about handling an emergency and enjoyed flying with me more. To be honest, having a spouse who also flies can be a negative since handing over the controls to another when you are used to being in charge is extremely unsettling, no matter how competent they are.

Things have worked out well, though. She loves to fly with me, occasionally takes the wheel if I am busy with the charts, but I do all the flying.

CHAPTER 3: CIVILIAN LIFE FLYING SAN JOSE

I loved the time I spent in the US Navy, but after considering all options, I decided to leave and open a private orthopedic practice in San Jose, California. I was drawn by the Mediterranean climate and the relaxed Western lifestyle. The skies were usually clear or only slightly hazy, with visibility rarely dropping below three miles. Many airports, both large and small, were accessible within a one or two-hour flight and opened up varied and beautiful locations to us. This marked a completely new chapter in my life, and flying out of San Jose became an entirely new experience.

Armed with a new wife who enjoyed flying, we could explore new horizons together. In the following chapters, you will see the world, or at least the environment, as we came to enjoy it: experiencing new adventures like camping, backpacking, rafting, hiking, skiing, and visiting relatives and tourist sites were made so accessible by air.

I started renting planes out of Reid Hillview Airport, which had two 3,000-foot runways, available fuel, and several flight schools in addition to plane rentals. Reid Hillview was only twenty-five minutes from my home and about five miles from the large commercial San Jose Airport. Later, after buying a plane, I relied on the mechanic at Squadron 2 at Reid Hillview for upkeep. It was more convenient and less expensive than the service at San Jose International, though I kept a tie-down at SJC.

Over the years, I bought several planes, each one filling the need of the time. The first was a Cessna 210 Centurion, a 300-horsepower, six-seat single-engine plane with retractable wheels. Mine had a STOL kit for short takeoffs and landings. It was practical, with enough power to carry six people and still handle any airport or grass strip.

Several years later, I joined a group of four pilots to share a Piper Chieftain, a ten-seat twin with 350-horsepower engines. It was not pressurized. This upgrade required me to take a special week-long course and earn my twin-engine rating. The downside was trying to fill the seats. Coordinating a group made trips more interesting, but it also required a lot of planning.

Insurance eventually required me to increase my twin-engine flight time, so I purchased a Piper PA-34 Seneca with 220-horsepower engines and six seats. It was a very practical plane, one I could take anywhere, and I felt secure with the second engine.

My final airplane, purchased in 1999, was a Cessna 340A with 315-horsepower engines, six seats, and pressurization. It was a cabin-class aircraft with entry stairs, de-icing equipment, radar, and state-of-the-art avionics for the time, including GPS. The limitation was that I would not take it onto gravel strips, which could nick the props and damage the de-ice boots. But the benefits far outweighed this drawback: increased speed, pressurization to fly above the weather, and the ability to use the higher winds aloft.

The Columbia State Park is only a one-hour flight from San

Jose. Judy and I would fly to its small airport, bringing our raft and paddles, then we would walk the quarter-mile dirt path to Route 49. From there, with paddles and raft in plain sight, we would hitchhike 5 miles up to a dirt road with a passing car or truck heading to the same spot along Rte 49. The Stanislaus River was famous for its 9 miles of heavy white water. Sadly, that came to an end when the New Melones Dam was built. The best part was that our car trip had to be done only once, while those who drove needed two cars; one at the top and one at the bottom.

At the end of our whitewater trip at Route 49, we would simply hitchhike back to the airport, usually with someone who had just run the river, and then fly home. In total, the time saved to make this great adventure was at least eight hours. Flying truly gives you freedom, both in travel and experiences.

Two of our favorite activities were backpacking and camping. In September 1978, we flew north to Happy Camp, a river town with a small airstrip in the coastal range just short of the Oregon border along the Klamath River. It was a one-and-a-half-hour flight up the Sacramento Valley. We enjoyed a weekend of hiking and camping, but by the last day, the weather had become overcast. My instrument ticket was useless here, as this remote mountain airstrip offered no instrument departures and trees bordered the runway's end. The clouds were positioned below the mountain peaks.

There was a small bar and shop at Happy Camp with the only available pay phone, as cell phones were not yet in use.

I contacted flight weather services, and the aviation weather representative immediately identified my location, likely due to either personal experience in the area or multiple previous calls from that establishment regarding local weather conditions. The long and short of the forecast was that this low-hanging cloud would not dissipate for days. The good news was that the weather in the Sacramento Valley was clear.

I like camping, but waiting in this camp was not my idea of a good time, especially with the weather closing in. At the bar, one of the locals told me some pilots would occasionally fly the river below the clouds to the valley, out of the mountains, where they could usually break out in clear weather or at least follow the roads. This was a bit of a risky option, but I knew the weather in the valley was relatively good, and if necessary, I could get an instrument clearance in the air and away from the mountains.

Pulling out the VFR sectional chart that showed the mountains, creeks, roads, and altitudes, I studied the map before taking off to fly down the Klamath itself to the valley and open skies. We both knew that if we somehow got lost flying low-level in the valley, there was not much of an escape route. I followed the Klamath River from Happy Camp as we wove through the mountains. The trick was to follow the river itself and not some offshoot tributary that could branch off into a blind canyon with little room to maneuver. With my nerves on high alert, I chose to fly close to the side of the river for a possible urgent turn while Judy scanned the ground for an emergency landing spot.

Finally, with a sigh of relief, we exited the mountains and fog into an open, wide valley, and I was euphoric to know the risk was over. I hate to admit just how many times I have felt this sensation over decades of flying!

By this time, I had about 100 hours, and it was time to buy my own plane, a turbo Cessna 210, N6765R, in April 1979. This Cessna had a STOL (short takeoff and landing) kit already applied to the wings, making it a short takeoff and landing modification. It was time to take it camping.

Our 300 hp, six-seater plane was ready for a camping trip to Idaho with our friends Brad and Dianne. We flew from San Jose and first stopped in Boise for fuel before heading to Johnson Creek, the planned area for camping. After takeoff, we heard the pilot who had departed just before us inform the tower that they were heading to Deadwood Reservoir, an airstrip about 50 miles north of Boise, marked with a question mark on the sectional map. I radioed the plane's call name, numbers, and asked about their destination. They reported they planned to land on the strip right by the reservoir and set up camp.

They cautioned me that the strip was a bumpy grass and dirt runway on the side of a mountain with about a 30-degree slope. Their advice was simple: "Touch down at the bottom of the strip and add power to get to the top." Otherwise, there would not be enough runway to fly out because the strip was only about 500 feet long. Since their plane landed, I felt I could do it as well, especially with the STOL kit.

As the wheels made contact with the ground, I applied full power, guided the plane over the uneven terrain, and reached the top of the strip. Wow. That was a unique landing, and I was more impressed that I actually did it without any problem. I found myself wondering why I had risked that strip at all, since I had no way to know the real length or condition of the runway only that the other plane had made it. Dumb decision, good outcome for now, since I had to risk the takeoff in a couple of days. Potentially a bigger risk!

For several days, we enjoyed the beautiful Idaho mountainous surroundings. When the time came to depart, the other pilot helped me turn the plane around for takeoff. I did a run-up on the engines, confident the plane would fly, and as I held my foot on the brakes, Brad removed the chocks and jumped aboard. Pointing down the airstrip, I took a deep breath as we bounced across the ruts, trying to keep the nose wheel from grabbing in a small ditch, gaining speed with no abort feasible. Finally, at takeoff speed, the main wheels left the ground just above stall speed. Still gaining speed and altitude, I now felt confident we would clear the small shack at the bottom. Yikes, I had performed another great flying job maneuver (feat?), though probably not a smart flying decision

Our Next stop was a grass strip at Johnson Creek, Idaho. Though unpaved and in the middle of nowhere, the strip was smooth and reasonably long. We camped not far from town and, before takeoff the next day, enjoyed their special ice cream.

The next flight for fun was to Chester, California. Only an hour and a half away, the unattended airport was right next to Lake Almanor and within walking distance. Judy and I went to the marina and rented a 16-foot catamaran. While I had previous sailing experience, this was my first time operating a catamaran. The differences between traditional sailboats and catamarans were yet to be explored.

The day was beautiful, the water calm, and a gentle wind blew. I adapted quickly to sailing this fast boat, which moved more quickly than any monohull I had previously sailed. As we progressed along, sometimes lifting onto one pontoon and leaning over the opposite side, I realized the conceptual difference between catamarans and monohulls, specifically regarding pitch-poling.

In a monohull, an error typically results in capsizing, which I had experienced several times. It is usually a gradual process. The sailboat leans slowly to one side as the sail tilts with full wind. The sailors lean opposite the tilt, enjoying the excitement, until one realizes the tipping point has been reached and nothing can stop the capsize. It isn't instant or traumatic, just slow motion as you get wet. On one occasion in a 20-foot Rhodes monohull, one of my passengers didn't even get wet; he simply rode the gunnel to the bottom of the boat as it inverted, staying dry. In that instance, the mast hit the bottom and got stuck.

On this day, in the catamaran, I watched the tip of the lee-side pontoon ride over the developing waves. The boat rocked fore and aft, and the tip drew closer to the water. The term pitch-pole came to mind. At the speed we were moving, if the lee pontoon dug into the wave, Judy and I would be projected over the bow like being shot out of a cannon. It was time to slow down. What a ride, before my thoughts of what could happen spoiled the moment.

This concept was always a worry when I used to land the Lake Amphibian in my Florida days. The plane, too, could pitch-pole if the bow dug into an oncoming wave, or if both small wing pontoons dug in at the same time.

Taking short trips around the San Francisco Bay Area in a small plane gave us opportunities to explore and camp at different sites, but there was always more to see. Our entire country is remarkably open to travel by private plane, especially compared to Europe.

In August 1981, Judy and I flew to Columbus, Ohio, on a commercial flight to attend her 20-year high school reunion. Since we were in the Midwest, we accepted a friend's invitation to visit her family's Canadian house on a lake in Parry Sound, North of Toronto. I rented a Piper Warrior, got checked out at the Columbus airport (CMH), and flew to Hamilton, Ontario, for customs. After refueling, we set out to find the Parry Sound airport.

We were flying VFR, navigating by ground reference. Remember, this was 1981, and there was no GPS for small private planes readily available. As we flew north into Canada, the weather started to close in, and after flying lower than I wanted in unfamiliar terrain, I requested an IFR clearance. Canadian radar in this isolated area was limited, so they couldn't pinpoint me, nor could I pinpoint the Parry Sound airport. At about 3,000 feet, in and out of the clouds and at the mercy of the winds, which were tossing us all around through a low-grade thunderstorm, when suddenly we found a window out of the clouds into a funnel-shaped sucker hole, and miraculously, we spotted crossed runways just below!

I called on Unicom, not knowing the airport frequency or what airport it was, and to my surprise, the tower answered, asking if I was Gordon. It was like music in my headphones! Canadian controllers had forwarded my IFR flight plan, and Parry Sound was expecting me. Spiraling down through that small hole in the clouds, I flew ever-tighter circles to stay within the opening and keep the ground in view until I could land at my destination.

Our friends picked us up at the little airport and drove us to Parry Sound, where we collected their small rowboat with an outboard motor. This was the only way to reach their cabin, which had no road access. The cabin had been in her family for more than a hundred years, and very little had changed. They had added flush toilets only a couple of years earlier.

It was a delightful setting, just steps from a peaceful lake. Kayaking in such seclusion is the best. Evenings at the rustic cabin with a bottle of wine, a good dinner, friends, and the sound of crickets could not be beat.

The trip back was also in the clouds, but at least this time there were radio beacons and an ILS system to guide us easily into Hamilton Airport.

In July 1987, Judy and I flew to Ashland for the Oregon Shakespeare Festival. This decades-old festival of Shakespearean and contemporary plays runs all summer, and Ashland itself is a quaint town, perfect for hiking, shopping, and dining. Our plan was to meet some old friends from the Bay Area who had driven up for business. Together we would enjoy the restaurants, see several plays over a three- or four-day weekend, and hike five to seven miles in the hills around Ashland each morning.

The airport was conveniently located right next to town, within walking distance of the hotel where we stayed. Since our friends had driven, we didn't need a rental car. The flight is only one and a half hours, far easier than their six- to eight-hour drive. For me, it was pure pleasure. On weekends, the street vendors set up along the roads, and I especially enjoyed seeing the woodworkers' creations, as I was into woodworking myself at the time.

One evening, as we walked toward the Elizabethan Theater, we noticed a young couple standing beside a curious-looking bicycle. It had handlebars and two wheels like a regular bike, but no pedals, with a suspended seat slung from an overhead arch. Intrigued, we stopped to take a closer look.

The contraption, called a Glydecycle, was designed to reduce weight on the body while running rather than pedaling.

As the curtain was about to rise, we couldn't linger, but the couple invited us to visit their hangar the next morning to see it properly. He was a pilot with a plane and a hangar, and as I often say, birds of a feather flock together.

The next day, we met them at the airport and tried the Glydecycle, riding around the taxiways until we grew accustomed to its partial weight-bearing feel. I loved the idea and ended up buying two. They disassembled easily and fit into the plane.

I had been running for forty years but was beginning to have trouble with my usual route. The Glydecycle made running possible again. Unlike a standard bicycle, which keeps the knees bent and rarely allows full leg extension, the Glydecycle permitted complete motion. After a standard bicycle accident left me with a hip fracture stabilized by a gamma nail, I needed crutches to walk. Yet within a week of surgery, I was able to run on park bike paths to this day, and I still run about four miles on it. By the way, I'm eighty-three.

Neighbors of ours, Jim and Adele, were both pilots and often rented planes. We planned a weekend trip together to Sunriver, Oregon, a resort about 400 miles north of San Jose with its own airport and convenient amenities like a courtesy van, rental bikes, and various lodging options. The area offers two golf courses, swimming pools, a river for canoeing or fishing, and is close to the Mount Bachelor ski area in winter, as well as good hiking trails. Despite the rainy weather during our visit, we enjoyed exploring the shops and scenery, and ultimately decided to buy a condo there for year-round use and potential rental income. We were drawn to the range of activities and practical advantages, as well as the opportunity to rent the condo to help offset expenses. Most importantly, this was a great excuse to take a trip and give me flying time.

Unfortunately, the inclement weather continued, so the flight back to San Jose was in the rain and was IFR most of the way. Once in the clouds, I realized the door on the Cessna 210 was ajar. It was no problem since we weren't pressurized, but it was awkward to get enough force to close the door while fastened to my seatbelt. Since my copilot was actually a licensed pilot, I told him to take the controls while I turned around in my seat to close the door. I didn't have an autopilot, and in those few seconds, my copilot inadvertently put us into a 40-degree bank, the sort of beginning of the death spirals one reads about occurring in the clouds, a la John F Kennedy Jr, many years later. We weren't near that, but I was amazed at how quickly a non-instrumented pilot can lose control in the clouds.

Since we had the condo and Sunriver was a destination for all four seasons, we made many trips there. One of the earlier trips included our children. My daughter was three, and my son Zach was one year old. He was riding in Judy's lap in the co-pilot seat as we proceeded up the Sacramento Valley in smooth air when, all of a sudden, there was a deafening silence. The engines had quit. Both engines. It took a few seconds to realize that Zach, who had been sleeping, kicked out his legs to turn over and knocked the throttles and fuel levers to the off position with his feet. Nothing like a little excitement to get the blood moving. For standard combustion plane engines, it doesn't take much to restart them since the props are still turning with the wind, but in jets, that's a whole different and very disturbing story.

In May 1990, we visited Sedona, Arizona, for my birthday. Sedona is known for its artistic community, multi-colored mountains for hiking, and beautiful desert landscapes. The mountains feature striking colors of iron ore and copper in the canyons, and the airport sits atop a mesa, making approaches unique. The elevation of the landing is actually about 500 feet higher than the ground below, which is used to calculate the final approach altitude. I was uneasy trying to make the necessary calculations while handling an otherwise normal landing. The placement of the runway atop the mesa with a sharp drop at the end, surrounded by colorful mountains, was so unique and beautiful that Judy filmed the approach the whole way in.

In July 1994, Judy and I flew to Sandpoint, Idaho, for some camping and hiking for a couple of days. From there, we flew to Kalispell, Montana, for more of the same. We rented bicycles and rode up the mountain on the famous, winding "Road to the Sun." This is a challenge for most bikers, but the views from the road high above the National Park are worth the effort.

The flight path home was to take us through Aspen, Colorado, so we stopped to see friends with a beautiful vacation home in the mountains overlooking Snowmass Ski Resort. Aspen Airport is easy in the summer, but if you find yourself departing at night or in bad weather, beware of the mountain not far from the end of the southbound runway 15. It was good to see it in clear weather, so when I returned one winter, I had a better perception of the dangers.

In April 1999, my good friend, Jason, a wild and crazy guy and always willing to go on adventures with me, joined me to raft the Snake River in Idaho. My five-man life raft folds up and packs into the Seneca quite easily. We flew to Bonners Ferry, Idaho, rented a car, and drove to the river, which seemed to be a great fishing spot for the locals. We hitched a ride up to the top of the river, inflated the raft, and dropped into the running water, untested and uncharted.

The water was crystal clear and moving at a relatively good pace, not the rushing torrents I have experienced using individual inflatables called Orange Torpedos on prior trips. This was a pleasant rafting trip, passing all the fishermen along the banks and on inner tubes, with their rods in one hand and a beer in the other. America at its best. We had so much fun that we were able to get another ride up to the top to redo it. A five-hour flight each way left us tired at the end, but it was well worth the adrenaline rush and fun.

Mendocino is a quaint little town on the Pacific coast north of San Francisco, only an hour and a half by plane. It has a nice airport and is just a walk into town. It is situated by the ocean, and the fog can make it hard to land at times, but for a day's outing, it is perfect for a flight. Wandering around the town with its history can be very romantic, and browsing in the stores can be enticing, especially if you are into early American antiques. Judy and I fell in love with a set of decades-old stained-glass door panels that had graced the doors of the long-gone Mendocino Hotel. Two panels, 24 by 60 inches, fit right into our plane, and we had them set into large oak doors for our home. Now, every time I pass through the doorway, I am reminded of that pleasant trip to Mendocino.

One of the most beautiful and unique places in the United States is Bryce Canyon, Utah. It is only 2.7 hours from San Jose, and the airport at Bryce Canyon is right by the National Park. Our landing in Bryce was a bit challenging when the airport was suddenly engulfed in a pretty turbulent rainstorm. On landing, I had to use every skill I possessed to keep the plane level as we touched down. My niece in the back was so relieved to be on the ground that she screamed out in delight. A car is necessary, but you can rent one right at that airport. Hiking in the canyon on a hot day can be difficult, but this August day in 1999 wasn't too bad. You have to plan to have enough energy and water, though, for the return hike, since you start at the rim and walk down deep into the canyon. Walking back up is much harder as the heat rises. We ended up hiking 10 miles within its spires and unique rock formations made up of multiple colors. It is a majestic place to immerse oneself.

When we got back to the plane, low and behold, the battery was dead! There are so many reasons for a dead battery, like a light left on and not noticed, or just an old battery that gave out. It was near the end of the day, but very fortunately, there was one guy on duty who had the right equipment to jump-start that fit my plane's electrical plug.

I've always worried about a dead battery, since I've taken my planes into the wilderness and very remote spots. The 24-volt battery is tricky, and you can't jump-charge it like the 12-volt batteries that are in single-engine planes. Most small planes have a 12-volt battery, so can they be started from a car battery? Unfortunately, the electrical plug may be near the propeller, which is a very scary place to be when fiddling with the power cord to start the props. My plan for a dead battery is, when there is no aviation shop around with the standard equipment, to use an adapter for the special plug in the rear of the right wing, well away from the props. I am able to connect two car batteries in series to jump the Cessna 340. Another tip: you really shouldn't charge it on the plane. A jump-start is one thing, but a full charge is another. Once the engines have started, they produce electricity so you can still have all the electrical equipment, including navigation and phones. If the battery died because the generators weren't working, that is simply bad luck.

In 1999, I fell in love with a historic, 100-year-old building in downtown San Jose, called the Letitia Building, and became involved as an investor with a neighbor, and was about to be renovated by one of the biggest builders in San Jose, Barry

Swenson of Swenson Builders, known for restoring old buildings.

Every year, Barry would throw a bash called The Low-Down High Tech Bonanza, and he would invite colleagues in the building business in the San Jose area, me included. Parents were encouraged to bring their kids filled with appropriate activities. There were several rowboats, some with small motors, and fishing tackle for the small, stocked lake. Since it is a ranch, there were horses to ride too. This was a general western hootenanny. He gave neat gifts to the kids; my son's favorites were the knives.

The ranch is about 10 miles from San Jose as the crow flies, but by car, it was about one and a half hours over windy mountain roads. The great part for me is that the ranch has a dirt airstrip, or rather a clearing, about 2,500 feet long, but could my twin land there? It wasn't enough to keep me away; I successfully landed without incident several times. There had been a serious accident there once, but fortunately, with no deaths.

In August, I took the family to Trinity Lake, a reservoir about 250 miles north of San Jose in the Shasta Trinity Alps. The neat thing was that there was a paved runway right next to the lake, within walking distance, and a public bathroom and an area to set up a tent right by the water. There were boat rentals with motors included, and it was a great place to fish, ride around the lake, or jump in for a swim. Once we rented a houseboat and spent a weekend water skiing. We went up often, and after a while, I found a KOA campground with better amenities that would even pick us up at the airport.

Once, coming in with my Cessna 340, the weather was getting iffy. I was VFR, and there wasn't an IFR approach available since the airport was well within the ring of mountains. I flew between the peaks, their tops covered by clouds, like flying in a covered canyon. To tell the truth, I was getting nervous and considering my options: turn around, continue flying VFR and hope the clouds stayed high enough to get through to the lake, or climb up, get IFR clearance back to another airport, and rent a car. The GPS with altitude readouts to nearby peaks gave me confidence, or at least backup against the lowering visibility. I wouldn't have continued to the airport without that newfangled electronic equipment. What a relief when I could finally see the lake between the mountain peaks, and I knew I could make it, but sweat was running down my neck with real concern.

One summer in 2001, Judy and I were invited to a relative's wedding in the LA area. The hotel where the event was being held, the LA Hilton, was within a mile of LAX. I made arrangements with the FBO Mercury Aviation, which was sold to Atlantic Aviation, to land at Los Angeles Airport and get transportation to the hotel. I was flying my Cessna 340, but I still felt intimidated by the other "hardware" on the field. Flying in from the north, VFR, I was directed to land on the north runway (24R), exit on Victor (taxiway), and hold before 24L. Ground control then cleared me to cross 24L, turn left on Delta, right on Papa, hold on 25L, and while on Papa, contact ground control on a totally different frequency. This was getting confusing.

Meanwhile, I was dodging huge 727s while crossing over to the south side of the airport. I got instructions to hold for one 727 while the commercial aircraft were told not to "step on that little Cessna 340." Finally, I made my way to the FBO after crossing the fourth parallel runway. I was treated exceptionally well there and given a transit car to get to the hotel, which we returned around midnight before flying back home to San Jose. What a great way to travel to a wedding 600 miles away for one evening, especially if drinking is not your thing. The only traffic we experienced had wings!

Looking back, I acknowledge that the experience of traversing a gigantic, busy airport is intimidating. A very unusual experience for most small plane pilots. All those pilots' eyes on my every move, the multiple directions for crossing active runways, and planes that couldn't stop easily if I made a mistake were all on my mind. The news often reports episodes of this happening, even to big commercial airlines that do this daily. A small mishap could cost lives. I was proud and relieved when I made it through without a mistake or a callout from ground control.

In March, the weather in San Jose was rainy, cold, and cloudy. My golf friends suggested we fly to Furnace Creek near Death Valley, within walking distance of the airport. Part of the adventure was the instrument flying, which in this case totaled three hours. The good and bad of flying in California is that the weather is generally VFR, and getting actual instrument experience isn't easy. When the occasion arose, I would take advantage. The golf game was just an excuse, but it made an otherwise unpleasant day enjoyable. The flight back was also at night, and getting nighttime experience never hurts.

In July 2004, my friend Rick and I thought we'd like to hike near Yellowstone National Park, Wyoming, and we would travel in two planes, each with our spouses. He owned a C210, and I had my C340, so we could take a group to go hiking. It took me four hours to reach KCOD; I can't recall Rick's travel time, but our hiking lasted three days. On the return trip to SJC, impressive clouds appeared to be coming out of the south, just like those in the Wyoming and Yellowstone photos. The forecast for these big, beautiful white clouds included not-so-beautiful thunderstorms.

Rick has his instrument license and is a very good pilot, which also means a very cautious pilot. Most of his flights had been from SJC to Truckee, where he had a second home. He used this home year-round, including in winter for skiing, but if the weather was iffy, he had no qualms about driving. Looking at the weather, there was no question what Rick would do. He stayed in Cody until the thunderstorm threat was resolved.

On the other hand, the reader has probably realized I haven't been tagged as an overly cautious pilot, given my logbook entries so far. I suspect that my days in Vietnam, flying around with some of the craziest but most competent pilots in the world, influenced my flying behavior. It also helps that my plane, well-equipped with radar and pressurization, is rated to fly in all types of weather, and I had confidence that controllers would steer me clear of violent thunderheads. We took off, weaving around the clouds VFR and climbing high enough to see the billowing thunderheads. I also had my radar, but I am always more comfortable with what I can see in front of me. Given my radar was aging (1977), I never really trusted it 100 percent. As it turned out, the ride was a bit bumpy, but I didn't have to avoid anything that looked threatening. Another calculated risk that worked out. Rick flew back comfortably in the clear the next day.

In July 2006, my sister Judy and brother-in-law David were visiting from Boston. As I wrote at the beginning of this saga, David was my inspiration for getting my pilot's license. He had been a Marine pilot, flying helicopters, and when he left the military, he took over his father's business of manufacturing and selling odd-sized tires, mostly for farms and trucks. He earned his civilian pilot's license with refresher lessons and later got his instrument license. Since his tire business catered to a large area of the East Coast and Canada, he used a plane to fly into small airports where farmers needed his odd-sized tires for their equipment.

He needed a reliable plane with two engines and bought an inline (front and rear engines) twin engine, the Cessna 337. The pilot didn't need a twin rating to fly it. It wasn't fast for a twin, with a maximum cruise of 172 knots but a key advantage of this inline configuration is that it does not experience the significant loss of control typically associated with wing-mounted twins when one engine fails. It was a safety feature, allowing the flight to continue, although slowly. The plane could climb no more than 300 feet a minute on the front engine, and not as well if only the rear engine was running.

Several years later, as his business expanded, David acquired a pre-owned Cessna Conquest twin propjet and upgraded his license to include a twin-engine rating. He subsequently sold his old Cessna 337 to a buyer who modified the aircraft by installing a camera through an aperture in the fuselage. The plane was then configured to photograph the melting ice of Greenland and similar places from the air. The new owner flew across the Atlantic many times in David's old plane.

In a random bit of coincidence, it just so happened that David's old 337 flew back into his life. It was on a trip with us, my sister, and niece up to Glacier National Park and then on to Calgary for the annual Calgary Stampede, a real hoot of an event. We had cleared customs, which in 2006 was pre-9/11, so it was handled only by phone. While I was tying down the plane, my brother-in-law suddenly began shouting and pointing. I wasn't sure if it was a catastrophe about to happen or if he was having a fit of some sort. It turns out he was pointing to a plane that had just landed and was taxiing to the ramp.

"I said, "That looks like the same type of plane you sold

several years ago." "No," he replied in excitement, "that's 'My Mistress', the very same one with the same call sign." The pilot maneuvered closer to our position, and David quickly noticed the modifications that had been made to the camera mount. We approached the owner, who confirmed that his aircraft had recently crossed the Atlantic, a trip he had made on several occasions. We were astonished that a plane of its size could manage such a venture. Even more surprising was that this reunion happened in such a random and remote spot, and we landed within an hour of each other. In the world of general aviation, there is never a dull moment.

Watching solar eclipse at Redmond Airport

On August 23, 2017, an eclipse was set to occur in the United States, with totality visible in Oregon, only a two-hour flight away. I packed the C340 with two couples and flew up to Redmond, Oregon (RDM), the only airport with available space for planes within a reasonable flying distance from San Jose. Many airports along the path of totality were restricting access to aircraft with prior reservations, but Redmond remained open.

The scene was remarkable. Planes lined the tarmac, and groups of friends and crew sat together, wearing their eclipse glasses and staring skyward. There was no disappointment. The sun and moon knew what to do, and they did it well. For about an hour, all heads tilted back as the "diamond ring" appeared at the climax.

CHAPTER 4: WINTER FLYING

Winter brings a whole other level of flying conditions, and in California, the sport of skiing is king. California doesn't always get the best snow, so flying to where the best snow is a wonderful option. With private flying, following the snow and changing plans is easy.

One of the reasons we bought a condominium in Sun River is its proximity to Mt. Bachelor, a well-regarded ski area that offers a diverse range of trails and typically receives substantial snowfall. There is no housing at the resort itself, and Sun River is one of the closest available accommodations. A bus runs to the resort about 20 miles away, though a rental car provides more freedom. Sun River Airport also makes travel efficient.

According to my logbook, 1989 was the first year I flew specifically for skiing, with several flights to this ski area as well as others with nearby airports. This was during the heart of the drought in California, and Tahoe had virtually no snow. We were anxious to teach our young children to ski, and this was the best option.

While snow conditions may be excellent, flight conditions can be questionable. The same storms that bring great skiing often bring hazards: airframe icing, strong winds, poor visibility in snow, and icy runways. Flying in mountainous terrain with ice accumulation poses significant risks, as the added weight degrades wing efficiency and aircraft stability. In such conditions, pilot vigilance must sharpen, airspeed must be monitored constantly, and altitude adjustments must be evaluated carefully to mitigate icing. Stall speeds under icing can be much higher than the numbers published in the pilot operating handbook.

I recall one flight in Northern California where controlling the plane suddenly became difficult. The aircraft felt sluggish, as if I were flying right at stall speed. It wasn't even severe weather, but the tail felt heavy, the wings seemed to be icing, and frost crept across the windshield. That was one of my "oh shit" moments. I knew I was in trouble.

I activated the deicing boots on the wings, and soon chunks of ice began breaking off, slamming against the fuselage with a loud bang. The first time I ever heard that sound, I thought something had broken, but I quickly learned it was music to my ears as it meant the wing "boots" were doing their job to break up the ice. The Pitot tube heater was on, keeping my airspeed indicator alive, which was critical; without it, I'd have no idea whether I was flying or falling out of the sky.

All of this can happen in about 15 seconds, though under stress, it feels much longer. The next step was to call air traffic control and request a change in altitude. Warmer air is usually found below, or sometimes above, if you can climb through the tops. In this case, I chose to climb. Being pressurized gave me that option, and I prefer climbing when in doubt because if you go lower and the ice doesn't shed, you may not have the performance to climb back up.

Early in my career, flying the Seneca, I was making a procedure ILS approach into Sun Valley Airport. The approach there runs through a valley straight toward a blind wall, not far from the runway's endpoint. All my anti-ice equipment was working: the pounding of ice hitting the frame, alcohol streaming across the windshield just enough to keep a view ahead, and the Pitot tube so hot it could burn fingers. I focused on staying on the electronic line of the approach and couldn't glance at the wings as often as I wanted. Still, with the descent keeping my airspeed stable, I felt relatively confident. Concerned, yes, but reassured by the smoothness of the flight.

After landing, I finally saw how much ice had built up, nearly four inches thick, on some of the antennae. Holy shit that was a lot of load. If nothing else, it gave me lasting confidence that the Seneca was one tough, reliable airplane.

In January 1990, I flew my Seneca to Salt Lake City for an orthopedic meeting on arthroscopy. This was a new technique at the time, and it was time to get trained. Crossing the Sierra Mountains, I had to climb to flight level 190 (19,000 feet) to stay above the clouds. Fortunately, the Seneca had oxygen, but the switch to turn it on was located in the back of the plane and needed to be opened before takeoff. The system leaked, so I kept it off until I knew I would need it. Once in flight, there was no way to climb into the rear, open the little hatch, and reach the oxygen tank. Pre-planning was critical, and this time I didn't have the foresight, as it was not part of my preflight checklist. Legally, a pilot is able to go above

12,500 feet for a short time, but staying at that altitude risks hypoxia. While in the Navy as a flight surgeon, I went through the pressure chamber and experienced hypoxia firsthand. It sneaks up on you. Before long, you lose your cognitive function and can even pass out. Thinking you can outlast it won't work.

Crossing the Sierras in winter with high winds is a serious matter. The peaks rise above 11,000 feet, and with 50-mph winds rolling over from the Pacific, the downdrafts, as much as 2000 ft, could take a twin-engine plane down, into a mountainside before you knew it. I usually climbed to at least 13,000 feet to account for that margin.   In this case, I had a tailwind and wouldn't spend much time above 13,000 feet. I felt the risk of hypoxia for a short time was better than the risk of the down drafts. As I expected, I had a quick sprint over the Sierras and little hypoxic effect.

One clear day, my partner, flying a C210 from Las Vegas to San Jose, couldn't cross the Sierras due to strong winds. He couldn't gain altitude, and his ground speed dropped dangerously low to around 90 kts. Turning back to Las Vegas, his ground speed shot up to about 250kts, while his normal cruise speed was 170 knots. That was one severe wind!

In December 1992, my wife and I flew to Telluride, Colorado, to ski. We left in the afternoon and made phenomenal time with a 100 kt tailwind, and as we approached about 20 miles out, I called the tower to advise them I was inbound. They asked for my expected arrival time. A curfew was in effect, no takeoffs or landings after dark, which was quickly approaching. At that moment, the tower had a 727 ready for takeoff, but because they were IFR and I was inbound, they couldn't release the jet until I landed. They were insistent that I hurry, and I wanted to get in before they closed the runway.

Telluride has essentially a one-way runway for departures. Takeoffs must be to the west, since a massive mountain wall blocks the eastern end. The west end, in contrast, drops off sharply into a cliff like a carrier launch. As I landed on Runway 27, the tower instructed me to exit as soon as possible. I took the first taxiway, and just as I cleared, the 727 whooshed past my tail. The tower immediately closed the airport. By then, it was dark.

Telluride is a great place to ski, and the town has kept its old cowboy motif. Very friendly, with a Western vibe. While we were there, Sylvester Stallone entered a crowded restaurant and expected to be seated immediately. The bartender and owner advised him, in no uncertain terms, that fame had no place in his establishment, and he could leave. Applause all around. That was the general attitude of this town. We were all important, whether rich, famous, or commoner. We also ran into Oprah at the little FBO, lounging in her sweats and unmade up, waiting for her flight out.

Skiing can be a strong draw, and in December 2010, the snow in Truckee was terrific. Flying up, the visibility was good above the 2000-foot layer of clouds surrounding the peaks, as is often seen at Truckee. I called the tower and confirmed the runway was clear, possibly a little icy, but visibility was good under the overcast. I had to take the GPS Z approach down to 525 feet, and as I broke out, the black runway 20, a comfortable 4650 feet long, was sharply outlined by a wall of white snow that had been plowed earlier, with the walls higher than the tips of my wings.

It seemed narrower than the 75 feet advertised by the approach chart. Usually, the wings overhanging the runway edges don't matter, but the snow buildup changed that thought. The landing was standard, but taxiing at first at about 90 mph down that black strip bordered by snow piled high from the plows was unsettling. The wing tips seemed dangerously close, and with ice on the field, any small deviation could catch one of my wingtip fuel tanks. Braking would only make it worse and would not slow me down or help in aiming the plane toward the center of the runway. Flying a twin, one learns that differential power on the props offers the best hope of regaining control of a slide. I was happy to reach the ramp and park.

Good skiing, great snow, and even while we were there, the slopes were excellent. Three days later, when it was time to return to San Jose, I had to dig the plane out of the ice cage I found it in. Not only was the plane covered, but the ramp and any way of getting to the taxiway were buried. Shovel in hand, I worked for hours to free the plane, let alone clear the ice from the wings. Since the plows had trouble clearing the runways and taxiways, I had to wait another day.

I had flown in and out of Truckee so many times that I figured I could do it blind. In December 2001, we flew up to Truckee to ski for several days, and on the 30th, after skiing, the visibility was quite bad when we got to the airport. In aviation speak, it was zero-zero. That means the ceiling was down to the ground, and the forward visibility was zero. Well, it wasn't exactly zero. I could see the white centerline on the taxiway and the runway.

Winter flying in Truckee, CA

The weather above the airport was actually good. There was no wind, no rain, just stars after breaking above the fog layer, only about 50 feet deep. I had once had a partner who told me he had taken off zero-zero. I figured if he could do it, I could do it, and this was the place. I was very familiar with this airport, and though it had mountains all around, I knew where they were. The runway was plenty long, and as long as I kept the nose up and my eyes on the artificial horizon, I would climb up through the overcast in no time.

I had my IFR clearance valid for only 10 more minutes, but there was no one in the tower. On the roll, I kept the plane on the ground past my usual 100-knot lift-off speed to be sure of a climb. Piece of cake, though those 50 feet of fog seemed thicker than expected. The white tips of the peaks never looked so beautiful as I popped out on top on a clear night, bathed in fog. I was ecstatic. I did it again at Truckee in March 2003. Practice makes perfect.

CHAPTER 5: ALASKA

It is the last frontier, and it is melting away. Flying in Alaska is like the old Wild West: few rules, and those seemed more like suggestions, or at least it felt that way. A major source of transportation, many planes fly around barren areas with few navigational aids and difficult communication. Airports are a luxury; airstrips are scarce, and landing wherever on land or water is the norm. This was and is the draw, and flying in Alaska exceeded my wildest dreams. If there is a place that requires thinking out of the box, Alaska is at the top of the list. I fell in love with the thrill of it and returned multiple times, sharing the experience with many of my friends and family.

Flying over Glacier Bay Alaska

In June, my friend Gerry and I flew commercially to Anchorage and rented a single-engine Piper PA-28 to explore Alaska. After getting checked out on the rental, we flew up to Whitehorse. Whitehorse is an interesting little town where the original 49ers first stopped on their way to the gold fields. The town featured the original paddle boat that transported travelers to Dawson after their ascent from Haines. Touring this vessel provided valuable insight into the experiences of early adventurers. We took the modern way and flew the Piper to Dawson. The airport was mostly gravel except for a small area where the planes would do a run-up. This section was gravel-free so that pellets would not nick the tail of the plane and damage the de-icing boots.

I loved visiting Dawson and returned several times, watching the town change. On my initial visit, the primary establishment was Gold Tooth Gertie's Saloon, which remained in excellent condition. The wait staff was attired in authentic costumes reminiscent of the 1890s. The saloon offered gambling, meals, drinks, and shows. At the time, gambling in Canada, as I understood it, was outlawed, but here it made money hand over fist for the town, which owned it. All the money from Gold Tooth Gertie's had gone into rehabilitating the town into a tourist destination, and they had done a fantastic job.

The rest of the town featured multiple broken-down, forgotten, and ill-kept homes and stores. Over the years, when I returned, the entire town had undergone renovation. The houses were freshly painted, in good condition, with flowers spread across lawns and window boxes. A dredging barge was located a few miles north in a slough.

The dredging barge had been stuck in the creek mud, with about 10 feet above the muck showing in what had once been the waterway it had dredged 30 or 40 years earlier. On my first visit, it was a decrepit barge with a rotting wood hull, mired almost completely in sticky mud. On my last visit, I returned to the same dredge, now restored to its original five-story height above the waterline. The mud had been dug away, and touring the barge was fascinating. Gold was the reason for Dawson's establishment, and it was still being mined when I last visited. The gold miners used high-pressure hoses to wash the gold off the cliffs right beside the barge, which was practical, if not picturesque.

From Dawson, we flew to Inuvik in the Northwest Territories of Canada. We crossed a landscape I had never seen before. There were millions of little lakes, like Swiss cheese holes in the tundra, which stretched in a consistent moss-green carpet as far as we could see. If the single engine failed, I had no idea how we would get out of that no man's land. It was disconcerting. No roads, no vehicles, nothing. Later, we learned the locals crossed this area in the winter on snowmobiles or dog sleds, but in summer, the tundra would not support anything heavier than a person, and even then, boots sank to the knee. No place to put a plane down.

Inuvik is a small outpost town just inland from the Arctic Ocean. When landing, the tower asked: "Land, ski, or float? "Referring to the choices of runways, even in June. The town was mostly built on stilts, including the sewer system. The heat from homes would melt the tundra and cause buildings to sink, and the sewer system would freeze if not heated. Not much to do in Inuvik, we had lunch and then flew to Eagle, back in the US, to go through customs.

On our way to Soldotna, we noticed a grass runway with a single plane on the ground. The map indicated an airfield named Arctic Circle Hot Springs. We decided to land, not knowing what was there beyond a grass runway and an intriguing name. We walked a short distance to the "resort," which consisted of a few small cabins and an Elizabethan-style house beside a very large swimming pool. The pool, almost the size of a basketball court, was fed by glacier runoff at one end and by a hot spring at the other. Depending on your temperature preference, you could get very comfortable. On June 21st, the longest day, swimming there at midnight with the sun still bright was magical. It was Alaska after all, and part of its enduring draw for me.

We flew to Soldotna, rented a car, and drove to Kenai. Since we had not planned on fishing during this trip, Gerry found a fishing outpost store, picked up gear, and, most importantly, directions to the best fishing spot on the river. The instructions from the outpost went something like this: "Go down this road and cross the bridge over the Kenai. Turn right on the third dirt road, which will not be named, then go past three more dirt roads and turn right on the next one. Go exactly 1.2 miles, pull over, and park. On your left, there will be a path. Take the path over the small hill, and you will see the river."

We followed the directions, and after climbing the small hill, to our dismay, we spotted the river lined with 40 to 50 fishermen casting their lines. In Alaska, this crowded scene is known as military fishing. When the salmon, especially Kings, run, both locals and tourists fill the riverbanks. On that first visit, the shoreline held fishermen, scattered campfires with fish frying, and strings of salmon cooling in the river.

On later visits, sentimental to me, the same spot had grown into more than just a riverside filled with fishermen. It had become a regular tourist stop with bathrooms, a bait shack, and a food stand. Progress, perhaps, but that first time I truly felt it was an Alaska adventure, not the tourist destination it later became.

From Soldotna, we flew back to Anchorage to return the rental plane, then traveled commercially to San Jose.

On June 4, 1988, I took Dr. Parkinson, a family practice physician, and his two sons to Alaska in the Chieftain, an eight-seat, twin, non-pressurized, cabin-class airplane that was shared by four other pilots. We loaded the plane with all our fishing gear, including waders, tents, and camping equipment. Even with only the four of us in this big plane, the weight and balance were reaching toward the maximum. Dr. Parkinson was no small adult, and his two sons, top athletic linemen on the high school football team, tipped the scales.

Our first stop was Bellingham for an overnight and fuel. The next morning, we flew on to Prince Rupert, Alaska, with an ILS approach. Since we never landed in Canada, we didn't have to go through customs. Prince Rupert was a typical Alaskan town. The area around the airport was just the usual main street lined up, one bar after another, broken up only by a barber shop or a fishing outlet.

From there, we headed up to Juneau and had to make an LDA (localizer directional aid) approach into the airport. The next day, taking off from Juneau, the weather was overcast at about 2,000 feet. I decided to fly VFR under the overcast, following the ocean visually until the sky opened up so I could climb on top, which wasn't predicted to be very high. I used the WAC (world aeronautical chart) map to navigate visually among the various islands. Trouble was, I couldn't find any breaks in the clouds, and all the inlets on the map looked alike. Not being familiar with the landscape, I was wandering around the islands, essentially lost. I couldn't even find my way back to Juneau. Everything looked the same, island after island, inlet after inlet.

I hate that "lost feeling," especially while flying. Just try reading a WAC chart with all the islands and inlets while looking out the window, trying to correlate the map with the visual landscape. Nothing seemed to match. My only real option was to blindly fly through the cloud cover until I broke out on top. I had about 10 miles of visibility under the cloud cover, so I could tell where the Island Mountains were. Full throttle, gain speed, then climb at a steep angle until the clouds fall below the plane. Success. Finally, clear above the clouds and on our way to Whitehorse.

I knew it was a calculated risk, not approved by any aviation regulation, but it worked. I guess I had been holding my breath during the climb through the overcast, and the relief was pure once the sunlight guaranteed visibility and distance from the mountains.

On the way back from Alaska, the coastal weather turned cloudy, and since the transponder wasn't working, I couldn't fly through Canadian airspace IFR. However, I could fly VFR inland. This was the route most single-engine planes fly, following the roads, and I believe there were better refueling opportunities. We stopped in Fort St. John before reaching Bellingham, and from there, it was back to the U.S. and normal flying.

In June 1989, it was another trip to Alaska, but this time I flew the twin Seneca with three buddies, four hours to Paine, Washington, for an overnight, then up to Ketchikan, Whitehorse, and Dawson. If you go to Alaska and the Yukon, a must-read is Alaska by James Michener. The history of the gold rush and the very places the 49ers passed through are right before your eyes. From Dawson, we flew down to Circle Hot Springs Resort for a swim and then on to the Kenai Peninsula for fishing.

On the way back, we stopped at Yakutat for gas. This is the only airport between Kenai and Juneau. The definition of barren is Yakutat. Not much around it except for water and mountains full of trees. Then it was back through Juneau and finally to San Jose.

In the summer of 1991, I had another chance to fly to Alaska with my nephew, Byran, and two others. I took the Seneca, with the four of us packed into the six-seater. The itinerary took us through Bellingham and Sitka, with a localizer approach at both Ketchikan and Sitka. The next day, we continued up to Kenai for more fishing in the usual spot on the Kenai River.

A visit to Dawson seemed mandatory to watch the progress of the restoration. I noted the improvements as the town continued restoration to its original look. Gold Tooth Gertie's remained unchanged, the "diamond" of the town, funding the effort.

Our next stop was Lake Minchumina, a fairly large lake in the middle of the state with no roads, only two runways. One was a good-length gravel strip, about 4,200 feet, and the other was a cross-runway, pretty much dirt and sand. I landed on the gravel runway, pulled off to the side, and we started fishing about 30 yards from the end of the strip.

It took a while to catch the first fish, a northern pike. Ironically, it was my nephew, who rarely fished, who scored the first catch, while my buddy Ron, a proficient fisherman with all the right equipment, didn't even get a bite. As we stood on the bank of the lake, a small boat with an outboard motor drew closer. Since this was the middle of nowhere, we were blown away to see anyone at all, especially one with a gun strapped to his waist. A bit alarmed, we watched as the boat approached, and it turned out to be a man and his son out for a day of fishing. Nice enough, he recommended that we fish at the south end of the dirt strip. "That's where the fish are." Since we really weren't catching much where we were, it was worth trying. Byron suggested that instead of walking down the runway, we taxi the plane. Good idea.

As I was taxiing the plane, all of a sudden, the nose wheel dropped into a soft sand ditch. I was quick enough to stop the engines before the props could strike the dirt. We were about halfway down the strip, stuck in the sand. We tried pulling it out by the props, the only way to move the plane, but the four of us couldn't budge it. The only option was to power it out of the sandpit.

We started digging pits beneath the props and carved a small ramp so the wheels could slowly rise to the level of the dirt runway. With no shovels, only our camping hand tools, the four of us dug like crazed miners sensing gold underneath. Overhead, dark rain clouds began to roll in. If it rained, the dirt and sand would turn to mud, and we would really be stuck. Finally, our plan looked like it might work, so I climbed in, powered up the plane, and slowly the aircraft moved out of the pit onto more solid ground. We taxied carefully, with Byran and Ron walking ahead to guide us so we wouldn't repeat the nose-dive into a hidden pit.

The two fishermen were right about the fishing. At the south end, we could practically hook the pike with bare hooks. Nearby, we came across a 10x10 canvas tent, likely left behind by some military unit. No one was there, but it provided good shelter. We set up our campfire beside it, and soon we were roasting fresh pike on a makeshift grill as the rain fell lightly outside.

We had no trouble getting out the next day, taxiing carefully back to the gravel runway. I returned to the same lake a year or two later in my Chieftain, this time landing only on the gravel. On that trip, we walked along the dirt runway instead. Accompanying us was a friend's 16-year-old son, who was experiencing his first camping trip.

With a rifle available, mandatory when flying in Alaska, we gave him the opportunity to shoot, not at wildlife, but at targets we set up. His excitement was contagious. I thought about how meaningful the experience must have been for him. Growing up, I had little, if any, outdoor camping experience. My vacations had been to the ocean beaches of New Jersey and Maryland. Watching this youngster discover the outdoors firsthand, I realized I was also rediscovering what I had missed in my own formative years, but clearly had worked to make up for ever since!

The next day, we flew to Nome with a stop at Manley, a remote Yukon River outpost where the mosquitoes were especially large and bothersome. Mosquito hats were essential. Surprisingly, the place was packed with young Germans canoeing up the Yukon River to the Bering Sea, a grueling journey given the conditions. After takeoff, following the Yukon River from above, I realized how complicated the route was with its numerous channels and islands, an easy place to get lost. For these German travelers, it seemed like a rite of passage.

Nome wasn't much of a city, as you might assume, but we

rented a car and drove down the shore, stopping to talk to some of the Eskimos who were permanent residents. All along the road, wherever there were homes or trailers, there were dog houses, dozens of them right beside the human residences. It seemed that every homestead had multiple sled dogs, huskies, or some variety of the species. Obviously, they were the means of transportation in the winter.

We stopped at a home where some teenagers were hanging fish on what looked like clotheslines for laundry. They were drying the salmon caught that summer. On the beach next to the home were dories, confirming from whence the fish came. The mother told us her husband was out hunting bear, which they would salt and dry for the winter. She confirmed the family had almost had enough fish, and one more bear would be enough for the upcoming season. This is the polar (no pun intended) opposite of the lifestyle in the continental US.

The flight back to Kenai gave us a night's sleep, followed by the long flight back to San Jose, 15 hours in all, with stops in Sitka, Ketchikan, and Seattle. Along the way, about an hour before landing at Ketchikan, I asked Ron, who was in the back seat, if he would pass up the urinal. He asked me, "Why would I want it?" Surely he knew why I wanted it, so I told him to pass it up. His reply: "It's full!" On landing at Ketchikan, I couldn't even make it to the terminal. I had to wash the nose wheel. Lesson learned next time, one urinal per person.

Over the years, the pattern was to leave San Jose on a

Friday afternoon and return the following Sunday, so I only had to take a week off work, which proved more expensive than the cost of the trip itself, given I had an office to run. The average cost of this trip over the years, including gas, lodging, and rentals, was ca. $5000/person. That's half the cost of plunking down for a week at an Alaskan fishing resort and offering so much more.

In July 1993, there was another trip to Alaska in the Chieftain. There were six of us fellows, and we flew into Gustavus from Sitka, a short distance to an unmanned airport. This airport had no tower, but it did have a self-service gas pump. It was also the airport where commercial flights from Sitka would drop off tourists who wanted to see Glacier Bay. A bus would take them to the Glacier Bay Lodge on the inlet, where they could board a ferry for the ride into and around Glacier Bay.

Having reserved spots on the ferry, we got a ride to Glacier Bay and set up tents in a campground just below the hotel. This was an adventure trip, especially for the other five, who rarely did any backpacking or camping. Since I had organized the trip, I wanted to expose my friends to the outdoors and to real camping, not glamping.

We rented canoes, and as part of the deal, paddled them across the harbor to the ferry boat, which was scheduled to leave at 8 a.m. to take us 60 miles up Glacier Bay. The canoes were loaded on the deck of the ferry, ready for the next morning. With everything prepared, it was time to fix dinner.

My friend Jason from my white rafting story had brought a huge, marinated roast, along with Idaho potatoes. He dug a hole in the sandy part of the shore, built a fire, and threw the food into the pit, covering it so it would smolder for hours.

Of course, we were in our drinking mode, waiting for dinner. Jason was not a chef; he was an emergency room physician, but that dinner was one for the books. I don't know if it was the taste, the moon, the mountains and sea, or just the anticipation, but it was certainly memorable. Finally, it was dark enough to crawl into our tents.

In the middle of the night, a storm hit, and we were all soaked. The tents weren't really waterproof, and the ground mats couldn't handle the water running underneath. Needless to say, everything was soaked. Not only were we soaked, but so was all our equipment, sleeping bags, and clothes. At dawn, we broke camp, loaded our gear into wheelbarrows, hauled them to the ferry, and climbed aboard. The plan was to be dropped off about 50 miles up the bay, where the glaciers began, then kayak for several days, camp along the way, and get picked up at the same spot by the returning ferry. This ferry did a round trip every day, 60 miles up and back, mostly filled with tourists. It was interesting to see the glaciers and animals along the way, but we were after something different. We wanted adventure, kayaking, camping, and being out in the elements. This day, however, the ferry was empty. The weather had been so bad that the commercial flight from Sitka, which usually brought in over 100 tourists, couldn't make it. We had the entire ferry to ourselves. Since everything was soaked, we spread it all over the rows of seats to dry so our gear would be somewhat usable for camping.

As we progressed up the bay, we picked up a couple who had been kayaking and camping for several days. When they boarded, they looked like drowned rats, absolutely miserable. They were so happy to finally be somewhere dry. But for my crew, it was the last straw. No way were they going to endure the same. These two campers looked so bedraggled that my friends just couldn't see enduring the same. I had mutiny on my hands.

Fortunately, the sky cleared, mutiny was averted, and I convinced them that if they wanted a flight home with me, they had better get off the boat with the kayaks at our drop-off spot. I was determined to have them truly experience this particular adventure called surviving wild Alaska - 60 miles from nowhere, no roads, no inns, no bathrooms, and no communication. I don't know why I had that impulse, except that, like a religion, once you are converted, there is the urge to share that religion, even when unsolicited.

Then the question was, how do we get off the ferry with all our gear and kayaks? Do we wear our boots, risking water overflowing the tops, or do we go barefoot? We even considered wrapping plastic around our shoes. After much discussion, we decided to wear our tennis shoes since they were already pretty wet.

There are no docks in Glacier Bay. The catamaran ferry simply heads into the shore until it cannot progress further, lowers a ladder to the gravel shore from the bow, and we get on the foredeck to hand off our tents, sleeping bags, cooking gear, and paddles. Then we manhandled the kayaks off. Now we were fifty miles up the creek, so to speak, with kayaks, no people around, no communication with anyone, and miles of beautiful mountains covered with ice. We had our maps, so we piled our gear into the kayaks and started paddling toward the nearest glacier. I've done a lot of camping, but there is no place like Glacier Bay for solitude, beauty, and the best of the outdoors.

Kayaking in Glacier Bay in the 1980s when the glaciers met the bay

Finding the right spot was not difficult, not far from a glacier. We set up the tent, got the fire pit started, and sat down with a tin cup of wine. Majestic scenery. With a little luck, a couple of whales might play just yards away. Of course, there might also be a couple of bears doing the same thing, but why worry and spoil the moment? We had the mandatory bear-proof containers for the food, which we were instructed to place one hundred yards from the camp. This was 1993, and we could kayak right up to the glacier wall, perhaps a sheer one thousand feet, and watch water gush from an under-ice channel into the bay, along with calving from the glacier walls. This created ripples, but nothing large enough to upset the kayak. We were close enough to hear the creaking of the glacier.

When the ferry comes to the glacier, the motor noise destroys the ambience. As kayakers, we had the best front seat, with a little risk. At least I felt little risk, but I underestimated the power of a huge chunk of ice splashing down, causing not just a ripple but a huge wave that could topple a kayak. We were lucky not to have that happen while bobbing close to the glacier. On a subsequent trip with my son, we learned the power of a calving glacier.

On that trip, we went back to Dawson and Lake Minchumina with a stop in Valdez to do a white-water rafting trip. This was a commercial raft with a guide and six of us paddling up the Lowe River. If you go all the way to Alaska, you just have to squeeze in as much fun as possible. From that trip, we returned home via Sitka, Ketchikan, and Bellingham.

I had taken another trip similar to the previous one with my wife and two friends. The four of us duplicated almost the same trip to Gustavus. We loaded the plane again and brought all our gear to the campgrounds at Gustavus by wheelbarrow to one of the furthest possible campsites. That afternoon, we loaded the kayaks on the ferry and crawled into our tents. That night, just like before, it rained, though not as badly. Getting our tents down and packed away with all the gear was better than before, but we still had to roll the wheelbarrows back to the dock through soggy mud. That's when my wife saw the lodge above the campground. She declared, "You mean we could have slept in a dry bed before this ferry ride?" It was hard to explain, except that I will save a penny whenever I can. Fortunately, my wife knows me well and doesn't hold grudges long.

The trip out on the ferry was pleasant, with nice weather in the morning. We were dropped off at Glacier Bay with all our gear. It was clear we weren't seasoned campers as we exited the ferry, but compared to the first time, we were improving. As we unloaded the kayaks, the visitors on the round-trip ferry leaned against the rails, watching us get off in what was essentially the middle of nowhere, except for a glacier, mountains, and water. This was wilderness. Three days later, when we were picked up, the captain told us that most of the passengers had been wondering if we would even survive. He confided that they had spotted a bear up the shore, walking toward the line of tents we had set up. For some reason, we never connected.

In August 2000, my nearly annual Alaska adventure was with my friend George, his sixteen-year-old son Adam, and my sixteen-year-old son Zach. We flew up to Gustavus, rented kayaks as usual, and took the ferry up Glacier Bay. We kayaked to one of the glaciers that came down to the water and pulled our kayaks onto the gravel just to the side of it. This glacier had an irregular wall where we were, not a straight cliff, so we could climb all over the outcropping. There was a shelf my son climbed onto while I stood directly below, admiring the ice formation.

After playing on the glacier, we decided to have lunch in front of a large piece of ice that had obviously fallen earlier. The chunk, about ten feet high and just as wide, gave us a place to lean against while we ate. Not long into our meal, a large crash shook the air. The ledge my son had climbed, directly above me, fell about fifteen feet. Perhaps his weight had compromised it? Shards from that ice ledge sprayed like small bullets, but we were protected by the ice boulder we leaned against.

It always helps to have a bit of luck. If the ice shelf had fallen while Zach was on top and I was below, or if the ice rock had not protected us, I'm sure the trip would have ended there and possibly our lives as well. It would have been disastrous. We had no way to call for help, no significant medical supplies, and no one nearby to hail. Other kayakers were few and far between, though there were some.

One evening by the glacier, as we sat around the campfire, George read us a Jack London story about an Alaskan hunter caught in a snowstorm. The tale described the hunter's struggle to survive after slipping through ice and wetting his boot, forcing him to build a fire or risk losing his foot. Listening to this classic Alaskan story under the multitude of clear stars and mountains perfectly complemented our own adventure.

Canadian Air Force intercept between Alaska and Washington State

The trip home from Alaska, the last leg from Sitka to Bellingham, was in good weather. About halfway between the Alaskan border and the border of Washington State, Zach tapped me on the shoulder and told me to look off our right wing. There were two Canadian interceptor planes. I got on the radio to call Canadian control to see what was going on. They advised me that I was in prohibited airspace and ordered me to land. I checked the charts but saw nothing indicating prohibited airspace. I was flying the coast visually, had done it many times, and never saw anything on the maps showing restricted areas.

I didn't want to land anywhere in Canada. Not only did my son not have identification on him, but I didn't want to land

and get called on the carpet, or whatever the Canadians might do. If I delayed long enough, I'd be out of their reach. I felt my chances were better in the air. I wasn't far from American soil, and I kept arguing with the air controller about being in good airspace. I was pretty confident they wouldn't shoot me down, but you never know. This was before 9/11, so I don't think I would take that chance now.

In hindsight, I am unsure if I filed a flight plan. Perhaps it was simply an unfamiliar plane over Canadian airspace, not necessarily restricted. I continued flying, and I never heard anything further, so I'll never know for certain. Flying VFR in Alaska often meant going without one, as routes were flexible and filing wasn't always possible.

An old friend of Judy's had qualified to rent a tugboat in Alaska and invited us to join him and his wife in cruising. They flew up commercially since they would be there for several weeks, but we could join them in Juneau for a weekend. It took eight hours with two stops to get to Juneau, and we were met at the airport with the tugboat tied up. This tugboat had one nice cabin and a much smaller cuddy-type cabin, but you can't be too fussy when you're the guest.

We cruised up the coast and stopped in Haines, then further up the fjord to Skagway. I had been there before by plane when it was very busy, but this time, with the tugboat, we tied up to the wharf, and no other boat was there. It was a pleasure to see the town without the crowds, enjoying the bars right next to the wharves. We staggered home, or rather back to the tugboat. The next morning, our little tugboat was surrounded by three of the largest cruise liners, dwarfing our vessel and blotting out the sun. Pouring out of these ships were thousands of overweight tourists eager to get to the little shops. We couldn't get out of there fast enough after having enjoyed a peaceful day and evening in Haines. We hit it just right.

That same year, Judy and I flew our friends George and Tamar to Kodiak, Alaska, not my standard trip. George and Adam were part of the near-death glacier experience described previously, but this time our wives were on board, and we made arrangements to board a boat out of Kodiak. That meant flying across the Pacific Ocean from Cordova, about four hundred miles. Most of that distance was over water, with only a small island, Montague, about midway. Just the idea was a bit scary, but as you can tell, I don't scare easily. That midway island was at least a breather, knowing there was some dry land available, even though only for a few minutes in the long flight. I had two engines, and what are the odds that both would quit? Still, I breathed easier when we were "feet dry," in Navy speak.

While in Kodiak, we boarded a boat converted for eco-trips. The captain, a former Coast Guard officer previously stationed in Kodiak, had decided to buy a fishing boat and start his civilian career. That didn't work out as he hoped, so he began a new enterprise: eco trips, exploring the islands around Kodiak. The live-aboard quarters weren't attractive, so he also set up rustic cabins on shore where we could stay, our choice. He arranged for us to fly in a floatplane to a river at the far end of the island, where a fish ladder assured us the chances were good the bears would be feeding.

It was just the five of us, the fifth being the pilot. The flight was beautiful, and the mountain goats were at wing level as we rounded the mountains. After landing on the lake, we were escorted to a ledge high above the river and the fish ladder. We were close enough for good pictures with a telephoto, but far enough for safety from the bears. Tamar, an excellent amateur photographer, had magnificent cameras and was assigned to capture shots for all of us. Clicking away, she was in heaven, capturing multiple grizzly bears standing in the water just in front of the fish ladder, swiping at the current, and pulling out salmon. From claw to mouth in one swoop, it was like machinery in action. Occasionally, a mama bear would toss one of the salmon to the cubs waiting on the shore.

After the flight back, our captain took us to his boat and offloaded the kayaks. We climbed in and paddled around the smaller islands and inlets, dipping our paddles into the crystal-clear water. Looking down, you could see the fish and the most colorful array of starfish you could ever imagine. Puffins flew in and out of nests on rocky slopes. Tamar was juggling several cameras like any serious photographer, one balanced on her lap and another hanging from her neck while shooting with a third. In all this glory, she forgot she was in a kayak that can rock with even a little wave or slight movement of the body. Splash, there went the camera with all the bear pictures! She followed it with her eyes through the clear water as it slowly sank to the bottom. What a bummer. The camera could be replaced, but those once-in-a-lifetime bear pictures were a different story.

The flight back from Kodiak over water again was concerning, but what the heck. I had done it once before without problems, and I was feeling confident and experienced. The flight was to Yakatak, further south along the coast, since we were heading back to San Jose. Yakatak is like an island on the coast, surrounded by little more than ice-covered mountains. No roads, few airports, and very far away. The weather was turning nasty, which I have already shown can happen in Alaska without warning. As I was coming in, now on an IFR clearance, I was told to circle. A very small, typical Alaskan plane was coming into Yakatak VFR, actually at tree-top level, and had priority to land. I hate circling, especially after a long flight and when fuel is getting low. Finally, it was my turn, and as I flew down the ILS, I was right on the numbers, proper altitude, and aligned perfectly, but I still didn't see the runway. My choice was to try again, but since I was flying as precisely as I could, how would things get better? To add insult to injury, fuel could be a problem if I chose to divert, with no close airports. But somehow, that VFR pilot had made it in, and I was sure he was a local bush pilot. With heart in my throat, I continued the approach and at about 100 feet altitude, the elusive runway came into sight for one of my smooth landings. Did I mention my landings over the years have been pretty darn good in all kinds of conditions?!

Flying into Ketchikan in August 2011, it was raining with low visibility. I had to take a missed approach using the GPS to runway 11 after failing to see the runway at 440 feet above the water. I went missed and returned for the ILS approach, which usually isn't as good as the GPS for the same runway, though in this case it did have a lower missed approach height. Just at decision height, at 200 feet, I saw the runway. This one sat on top of its own mesa above the water. I taxied to the ramp, had lunch, and had the fuel people fill the tanks. We were continuing on to Sitka.

With full fuel and bladders empty, I taxied up the elevated ramp and down the runway for a takeoff to the southeast. It was still raining, though the overcast was a bit higher than at landing. I pushed the throttles forward, lifted off, and climbed into the clouds. At about 600 feet altitude, both engines lost power at once. There was just enough time for the usual "Oh shit." Actually, multiple "oh shits," which came in chorus with my friends on the plane. It lasted only seconds, with virtually no loss of altitude, and the engines came back, allowing us to regain altitude. In those few seconds, I was already contemplating where and how to land: straight ahead, wings level, in control, and with airspeed above stall as we descended through the clouds. There was no other choice, but we had a reprieve. Once the engines reignited and we were on our way, there was no reason to return to Ketchikan, which would have meant another low approach. I figured the cause of the momentary loss of power was water in the fuel tanks. The plane was refueled while it was raining. For both to quit at once, that had to be it. The rest of the trip was uneventful, except for wiping the sweat off our brows.

In the news in 2025, the 747 jet that went down in India just after takeoff lost power in both engines from complete fuel starvation, and the pilot couldn't restore it as quickly. With jets, the engines cannot respond as quickly as internal combustion airplanes.

On another venture into Alaska, I decided to visit Seward, situated at the end of a deep fjord. There were the usual clouds around the mountains, and I chose the GPS approach. Visibility was good below the clouds, and the ceiling at the airport was a couple of thousand feet. The flight path down the magenta line (color of line on GPS map display) ran through a narrow valley of tall snow-covered peaks, and the peaks I was able to glimpse through breaks in the clouds as I descended along the path were spectacularly close and beautiful. After descending out of the overcast, under 4,000 feet and about four miles from the runway, it looked pretty straight ahead to runway 16. Piece of cake. I lowered the wheels and aimed for the landing spot.

At about touchdown, I noted out my left window a very long runway, RWY 13, 4,533 feet long, coming into view. The mountain nearby had blocked the view until then. With no ability to make the 30-degree change in course at my current altitude, I continued toward RWY 16, knowing it was obviously shorter, though I didn't know how much shorter. It looked really short. After the faithful "oh shit," and inability to turn 30 degrees left to reach RWY 16, I continued straight ahead for

RWY 13. With full flaps already down, I pulled the throttles back, and as soon as the wheels touched the pavement, I stood on the brakes. The runway was 2,289 feet long. My usual limit for runways was 3,000 feet, and when I land at Reid-Hillview with that length runway, I normally use the entire runway without burning the brakes, though I always make sure to land as close to the approach end as possible.

Seward is a pretty spot in a fjord surrounded by those spiked white peaks. We rented kayaks and paddled to the point of the fjord where there are remnants of a WWII fort. The paddle out there was one of the exciting parts of the trip. Just about ten yards from my kayak, swimming parallel to me, were a couple of orcas that had just surfaced. At first, I was deeply concerned, but since there wasn't much I could do, I resolved to enjoy the moment. If attacked, I wouldn't have had a chance, so I might as well take it in. Fortunately, I think these Orcas were the vegetarian variety.

Further excitement came when my friend capsized his kayak. He swam to mine and tried to climb aboard. He hadn't paid attention to the instructional video we were both required to watch before renting the kayaks. In no uncertain terms, I told him to swim back to his own boat, climb in as instructed, and then I would get his paddle. My motto: if all else fails, read the instructions, or at least pay attention to the instructional video.

Over the 12 or more trips I flew to Alaska, I think I experienced just about everything possible except confronting a bear. Strangely, my bear sightings were just that and nothing up close and personal. Perhaps some of that is good bear-proofing of our campsites so as not to be enticing? Or just luck? As the reader can see, planning, smarts, instincts, training, and calm under pressure can only get you so far. Luck has been a big part of my life.

.

CHAPTER 6: AFRICA

For many years at aviation events, I would stop by the booth of Hank's Aero Adventures, a travel agency specializing in setting up pilots to tour South Africa in rental planes. His company arranged for us to rent aircraft, plan routes, and self-fly across the lower African continent, with all the logistics handled so we could move smoothly from safari camp to safari camp. I had been intrigued for several years but never committed.

In early 2003, Hank called and asked if I wanted to join a group of seven other pilots who belonged to a California Malibu flying club. This club was made up of owners of the Malibu, a single-engine, high-performance, and expensive airplane typically flown by very experienced pilots. Because this was such a large group, instead of creating separate itineraries for each plane, the eight pilots would fly together as a group. Best of all, Hank and his wife would lead us in their Helio Courier, which they had flown all the way from Salinas, California, to set up their business in Johannesburg, South Africa. Since private aviation is more restricted further North in Tanzania and Kenya, our focus was on the southern countries of Africa, where general aviation is permitted.

The route would take us about 1,200 miles: through South Africa to Botswana's Tuli Block and the Okavango Delta, then into Zambia along the lower Zambezi River and Victoria Falls, on to the lake region of Namibia, and finally back through Kruger National Park on our way home. I thought it was a perfect plan. Flying with someone who knew all the ins and outs of aviation in Africa offered real security, including potential technical issues, and sharing the experience with fellow pilots would make the journey even more enjoyable. The group had picked August because it is the end of winter with consistent weather and thinner brush for better animal viewing.

In August 2003, Judy and I flew commercial to South Africa. The group gathered at a hotel in Johannesburg, where we had an outdoor cocktail party to introduce ourselves. I wore a windbreaker embroidered with "USA 76" and "Oracle" beneath the logo. One of the guests immediately recognized it and said he had the exact same jacket. That surprised me since it was a rare piece of clothing. It was a gift as a part of my being asked by a friend to join the crew on Oracle's America's Cup sloop for a race on San Francisco Bay. As a sailing enthusiast, I was thrilled, and the team issued me this jacket, one of only a handful given to the crew. My new acquaintance knew it was genuine because his daughter worked for Larry Ellison, and she snagged him the same jacket. The coincidence struck me hard. The world can feel incredibly small at times.

We were joined by our friends, Brad and Diane, the same couple who risked the Deadman Reservoir landing in Idaho with us years before. Guess I hadn't scared them enough. I chose the C210 because I knew the plane well, it could carry four people, and it was available.

When we first signed up, Hank sent us a tremendous amount of material about flying in Africa. It included audio tapes of air traffic controllers so we could accustom our ears to the South African accent over the static of radios and the noise of engines. He also provided multiple maps: airspaces marked in colors for easy recognition, exact headings between each airport, radio frequencies, and photos of ground structures with distances noted.

This was before GPS was common, and VFR frequencies were scarce. There were few roads or rivers to follow for navigation. Every morning, our group gathered over breakfast to review the route for the day and discuss what to expect. With limited landmarks, poor communication, and few navigational aids, getting lost was always a possibility. On one leg, one of the planes did lose its way, and the rest of us felt a wave of apprehension until Hank located it again. We all knew it could just as easily be us next time.

On our first preflight briefing, Hank, the group's leader, advised us all to wear jackets with captain's shoulder stripes to indicate that we were professional pilots. The people traveling with us would wear jackets with three stripes to designate them as crew. This would help smooth border crossings, avoid some tourist fees, and generally make the process easier. He also recommended carrying only a light bag when checking into customs, leaving the rest of the luggage on the plane. Officials rarely inspected the aircraft of "working" pilots and crew.

After breakfast, we started our planes, all nine of them, and lined up for takeoff. The sight was both impressive and exciting. One after another, we lifted off from Lanseria, Johannesburg, climbing into the clear African sky. Our first stop was Limpopo, Botswana, FBLV, elevation 1,770 feet, with a 4,900-foot paved runway. The note on the chart read: Watch out, animals may be on the runway.

Like a flight of geese, the nine airplanes followed one another, each at different speeds and altitudes, with Hank as head goose. Flying a C210, I was the fastest, and because of the thermals, I chose to fly higher than the C182s and C172s, which kept me above the bumps. It made for a much smoother ride compared to what the other planes endured. That became evident when we landed; those at lower altitudes were more exhausted from the heat and thermal turbulence. The extra couple of thousand feet of altitude didn't diminish the view of animals below, although they looked to be tiny lumps at our altitude.

After landing at Limpopo, a van took us to the Mashatu Game Reserve Lodge. We were welcomed by the entire staff and escorted to our surprisingly luxurious cabins. Most of our accommodations throughout the trip were similar: airy, clean, and charmingly decorated in an African motif. We rarely stayed in tents, but when we did, they were also comfortable, one built on stilts so animals could pass beneath without disturbing us. Meals were both scrumptious and unique. Days were warm, evenings a little chilly.

In one tented camp, when I slipped under the covers, I felt something soft and warm against my feet. For a moment, I thought an animal had joined me in bed, but it turned out to be a hot water bottle placed there by the maid before we returned from dinner, an African version of an electric blanket, or the small chocolate left at turndown in modern hotels.

If you want to see wild animals, and that is the essence of a safari, Mashatu is ideal. They boast the "Big Five" – rhino, water buffalo, lion, leopard, and Elephant. We ended up seeing all. We were taken out in open-air safari jeeps, all eyes scanning constantly, following the driver's gaze to spot these and many other creatures. The reserve offered remarkable diversity, including canoe trips through large swamps where crocs glide stealthily by with only eyeballs gleaming above the surface. One incredible incident of a rare animal viewing occurred when we sneaked through the brush in our van to witness two elephants mating. Most remarkable was that the act was being celebrated by a parade of females circling to ward off any lion, or perhaps another bull elephant, thinking of taking advantage of the situation. Our guide of many years said this was a first!

Each leg of the tour was memorable, but the most striking was flying into Livingstone near Victoria Falls. The landscape from Lusaka to Livingstone was flat and monotonous, just miles of scrub. I knew we were headed to a world-renowned waterfall, but as my navigation showed we were nearing the falls, the landscape was unremarkable. The weather was clear, visibility unlimited, yet all we could see was what looked like a line of steam rising above the ground. I began to wonder if my reckoning was badly off.

Suddenly, we passed directly over the falls. Instead of a cascade of water, Victoria Falls revealed itself by a line of water vapor rising above a crack in the earth like a curtain. Flying directly over the falls, one sees the Zambesi River plunging down in spectacular fashion. It was breathtaking. I circled multiple times, taking the required photographs.

*Victoria Falls
Zambia*

*Photo by:
Gordon L. Levin, MD*

Victoria Falls, Zambia

Along the Zambesi in the afternoon, Judy and I walked to the base of the falls, looking up at the water spilling from the plains above. We were able to stand surprisingly close to the flow before it dropped into the river gorge. Later, along the Zambesi, Judy and I had dual massages in a tent open to the river, hippopotami roaring nearby in the water. Before beginning, the massage therapists held out their hands. At first, we had no idea what they were showing us, but later we learned they were demonstrating that they had no cuts that could pass on Aids germs.

The next safari camp was a short flight down the Zambezi River to the Zambian side of the river, across from Zimbabwe. Set along the banks, we canoed among the hippopotami and crocodiles, praying our guides knew what they were doing despite the obvious risk involved. Hippopotami can be very dangerous if aggravated, and viewers of nature channels know that crocs can also be an issue. Our guide later shared a story from the week before: a crocodile grabbed a little girl's arm as it hung over the gunnel of their motor boat, dragging her into the water. Another crocodile latched on, and in front of her father, she was torn apart. Here we were floating along in a small canoe, with crocodiles swimming nearby and hippos lining the banks. This place isn't Kansas!

Most of the airports we landed in were paved, but one was much cruder, mostly dirt. On final, about thirty feet above the runway and ready to touch down, I spotted a ditch cutting across the runway, maybe eight hundred feet ahead. I quickly altered plans and extended my intended touchdown point. Had I not seen that ditch, I'm sure we would have nosedived and flipped.

This airport wasn't unsecured from thieves but from wildlife. We were advised to place acacia branches with thorns around the tires to prevent hyenas from chewing on them. Their sharp needles are one of the few things to discourage a voracious hyena. Taking off from this strip required waiting for a staffer to drive giraffes off the runway.

I may be prejudiced, but I strongly feel that a flying safari is the best way to see Africa: efficiency and speed, views and perspective, and variety, not to mention the joy of flying. Hank's Aero Adventures was an excellent choice for us.

CHAPTER 7: CROSS COUNTRY

I had driven across the United States several times, but I wanted to fly over it myself. On July 23, 1987, Judy, the kids, and I flew across the country in the Seneca. The total time to Missouri was nine and a half hours, and we were going with the usual westerly winds. After a pleasant visit, revisiting our residency friends, we were off again. Next stop, Elkins City, West Virginia, to refuel, and then onward to Ocean City, Maryland.

The kids were getting pretty bored by all this flying and started fighting, making noise in the back seats. This unhappiness had to stop. The easiest way was to fly a little higher, over 12,500 feet, to deplete their brains of a little 02 to quiet them down. The hypoxia didn't inflict real brain damage, but it did make the rest of the leg pleasant. Ocean City was a beach stop not far from my original home in Silver Spring, Maryland.

When we were ready to continue to the next spot, I noted during my preflight that the left wing fuel cap was missing. Someone had apparently stolen it. I had parked at an FBO, and I felt they were responsible for this theft. The value of the fuel cap was minimal, but it was certainly a necessary part of the plane to fly. Without the cap, the venturi effect would drain all the fuel in a short time. Good thing I caught it, since I usually fill the tanks upon arrival at an airport. Where do you get a fuel cap? How long would it take? I can't remember how I convinced the FBO operator to take a cap from another plane, one that he knew wasn't going to fly soon, and then buy a new one later. Thankfully, we could be on our way

The next leg was up to Westchester, New York, where we visited my wife's best friend and maid of honor at our wedding. The following day, after a quick visit, we flew to Parry Sound, Ontario. This was my second time at this airport, and this time, to my relief, it was all VFR and not the hairy flight of a couple of years ago.

Several days later, the return trip took us back to Columbus, Ohio, to visit Judy's family, and then home by the northern route through Sioux City, Iowa, to Rapid City, South Dakota, with a side trip to the stone faces of four presidents at Mt. Rushmore. Flying around that monument is so much better than standing with the crowds looking up. The perspective of the surrounding mountains makes it stand out. Truly a masterpiece.

On July 4, 1990, Judy and I flew the Seneca to a sports medicine meeting in Hilton Head, South Carolina, stopping first in Lenexa, Kansas, to visit my brother. He often complained that the family never stopped when flying over in commercial planes, so this visit settled that. The return route took us through Jackson, Mississippi, and then Flagstaff, Arizona. While flying over Arizona's plains, I had excellent visibility and could easily spot thunderstorms. The reports from the flight service did not always match what I was seeing. Their suggested detours sometimes steered me directly toward storms, which made me appreciate the value of flying VFR and left me wondering about the risks of flying IFR in clouds.

In June 1992, it was another trip across the United States. First stop was Columbia, Missouri, to visit my Navy buddy, an orthopedic surgeon, and his wife. It is always a gift to have friends across the country, people who offer not only a place to stay but also companionship and memories. The next day, we flew on to Jacksonville, Florida, to see Larry, an ENT specialist from my Navy days in Oakland. Larry and I had been transferred to Jacksonville Naval Air Station at the same time in 1975. Judy, my girlfriend at the time, had met Emily at the public broadcasting station where she worked, and arranged a date with Larry. On that first date, Larry wore a tie, believing an East Coast woman would expect formality, while Emily dressed down in jeans, expecting Larry to embody the casual California style. Despite the crossed expectations, the date worked, and by the time of our visit, they had been married for fifteen years.

Returning to Jacksonville felt like stepping back into my youth, with the carefree life Judy and I had once lived in a rental house on the river, complete with a dock, a sailboat, and a motorboat. We enjoyed sailing in Larry's sailboat on the St. John River again. The rhythm of those days returned easily, even down to weathering a thunderstorm on the river, just as we had years before.

Our trip home to San Jose followed the southern route: Lafayette, Louisiana, then Albuquerque, New Mexico, and finally back to California. Flying through the South, thunderstorms were everywhere, a constant reminder of how fortunate we are with the weather in California. The controllers kept me safe.

As was mentioned in a previous chapter, both kids attended boarding schools in hidden corners of America with out-of-the-way airstrips and remote terrain in some cases. It burned up a lot of fuel flying at and used all my skill flying to places ranging from Coeur d'Alene, Idaho, Mt Pleasant and Provo, Utah, Gooding, Idaho, and Kalispell, Montana. One school, Montana Academy, was reached by an airport.

This involved many flights at all times of the year into far-flung locations, ranging from Coeur d'Alene, Idaho, to Mt Pleasant and Provo, Utah, Kalispell, Montana, and Gooding, Idaho. One school, Montana Academy, was reached by an airport, MT53 that sat twenty-two miles west of Kalispell. As luck would have it, the property itself had a small grass airstrip. When I landed the Seneca there, the other students were having a picnic nearby and were thrilled to watch us bring in a twin-engine plane on what was essentially a farmer's backyard strip. I was thrilled too. It was no small challenge.

Another trip was to take our son to a school in northern Washington State. That round trip was 10.6 hours in one day. The final leg over western Washington was at night, and I was tired. I was flying the Seneca VFR, but might as well have been IFR. It was the blackest flight I had ever flown, not a single light on the ground for hundreds of miles. Night flying is usually relaxing. Other planes are easy to spot; there is no sun or glare, and transmissions are few. This felt plain lonely, in an eerie sort of way, and I found it helpful to have an IFR rating.

One such flight was to Kalispell, Montana, to pick up my daughter from Montana Academy for Christmas. Arriving at night in heavy snowfall, I had to circle for 30 minutes since another pilot was making an instrument approach, probably a young delivery pilot logging hours for airline qualification. Most of those 30 minutes were spent convincing my wife that all was normal and nothing to worry about. At the same time, I was trying to convince myself.

I have to hand it to those delivery dogs, fearless just to get Amazon products to the little towns, as they spent hours to qualify for the commercial airliners. I was wondering what I was doing up there, too, flying circles in a snowstorm. Sometimes you feel much better on a dark, snowy night that there are others taking the same risk.

There was no one at the airport, no tower controller, only instructions from some distant facility. In other words, there was no one to define what the runway looked like. I expected that the other pilot would announce his landing at Kalispell, but he probably landed at another airport.

I finally got my clearance and went on the final. As I approached the landing, I had to turn on the runway lights with the appropriate frequency from my cockpit. This usually really defines the runway. Not this time. As the plane's landing lights came on, all I could see was snow. I followed the ILS to minimums, 200 feet above the ground, before I could see faint glows marking what I figured were the sides of the runway. Over the night, about a foot of snow had covered these lights.

When I landed, I wasn't even sure my wheels were on the ground; it was such a soft landing on at least a foot of snow. I didn't need brakes; I needed power to get the plane off the runway and to an area that I thought was the ramp, where I could leave the plane. The place was abandoned, but the rental car was waiting with keys hidden. If memory serves, the drive to the hotel in the blizzard was as hair-raising as the landing! Another unique flying experience to add to my repertoire.

In July 2021, we flew back to Columbus for Judy's high school reunion. The trip was fun, reliving adolescent years, and since we had made it all the way back east, we wanted to take advantage and find somewhere interesting. At a local store, we flipped through brochures for nearby tourist spots. One listed Mackinac Island, a small, historic island in Lake Michigan that we had never heard of. Even better, it had an airport. It felt like a discovery. We landed on a 3,500-foot paved runway, just 1.8 miles from the center of town.

The first thing we learned was that there are no cars on the island. Horse-drawn wagons provide the rides. The town has preserved the feel of the time of the War of 1812, much like Williamsburg, Virginia, with most accommodations still in that era's style. One can sit on the veranda of the Grand Hotel with a mint julep or wander through the historic homes.

As a physician, I was struck by the story of a trapper who was accidentally shot but survived a penetrating abdominal wound. The bullet hole in his stomach never closed, and as repayment to the physician who saved him, he allowed a series of experiments. This was the beginning of gastroenterology.

On our return from Mackinac Island, we flew the northern route through Regina and again to Calgary to re-experience the Stampede. Every year over the July 4th weekend, Calgary is alive with this thoroughly Western experience. During the day, you can wander through stalls of enormous farm livestock, then watch rodeos, wagon races, circus stunts, and horseback lancing under the pole tents. Everywhere there are thrills: magicians hypnotizing volunteers, bicycle stunts, motorcycle racing, high-wire acts, and wild performances. It's a great supercharged Western experience.

On the trip previously mentioned to Judy's high school reunion in Ohio in 2011, we wanted to take advantage of having made a long trip to the East and find somewhere interesting to add to the trip, so we continued flying west through Canada to Lake Louise and Jasper. In Jasper, we hiked along a beautiful creek and stayed the night, but at Lake Louise, we only passed overhead. From the air, the grand Fairmont Chateau Lake Louise looked magnificent, set against the turquoise water and mountain peaks. It was impressive and no doubt expensive. We told ourselves we would splurge next time, but we never made it back.

CHAPTER 8: MEXICO

Flying in Mexico is a unique experience because of language differences and various regulations, both formal and informal. I had to make sure I had all the necessary paperwork: the plane's title for proof of ownership, a notarized letter if renting or borrowing, my passport, pilot certificate, and medical certification.

A friend had just returned from Cabo San Lucas, where he and his wife decided on a whim to buy a one-week interval of a unit at a resort just beginning construction called Club Cascadas de Baja. I teased him about buying in Mexico, especially since in those days an American could not own property outright. That has changed since then. He said that to promote this new resort, he would arrange for us for three free days of a "look-see." I laughed and said I would only be interested if we could spend a week, since the flight down was long and a lot of fuel. I was excited for the chance to fly to Mexico. Well, by the end of our complimentary week, we loved the charm of the architecture and setting so much that we purchased two weeks of our "Margarita" unit, one in the fall and one in the spring.

First, you must cross the border. I typically flew into Mexico from San Jose, California, using points of entry like Tijuana, Mexicali, San Felipe, or La Paz. Each had its own advantages depending on the destination. When I first started traveling, I often stopped at Tijuana for customs and fuel, but the process could be difficult and frustrating.

After landing at Tijuana, the usual procedure was to taxi the plane over to the fueling station and have the personnel fill the tanks. While waiting, I had to walk to the customs office to show that I was not bringing any illicit products into Mexico, pay the entrance fee, and then obtain permission from the commandante to complete the entry process. Unfortunately, each step, fueling, customs, and the commandante's office were located far apart, requiring a considerable amount of walking.

Once, I could not enter Mexico because the required customs stamp, a simple rubber stamp, was missing. Without it, the authorities in Tijuana refused to let me leave, insisting that the stamp be on my paperwork. After the airport personnel searched the air base for an hour and a half, someone finally found the stamp in a metal box in a car's glove compartment. That experience, early in my trips, convinced me to avoid passing through Tijuana due to the inefficiency.

The other options were slightly better. Mexicali was a bit more efficient, and flying there allowed me to avoid the San Diego airspace and the constant air traffic control vectoring that came with it. Another choice was to stop at Calexico on the American side of the border, refuel, and then fly to San Felipe to go through customs and refuel again. Still, I was always nervous flying into Mexico without having passed through customs near the American border, just in case something happened between the border and customs.

Most of my trips were to Cabo San Lucas. When I first began flying there, I would refuel at La Paz and then continue on to Cabo San Lucas Airport. The flight was only twenty minutes, which saved fuel by avoiding another climb. La Paz was also an international airport, and since departures from Mexico back to the United States required leaving from an international airport, it was convenient until Cabo San Lucas itself became international.

Circling Cabo San Lucas to signal for taxi at local airport

Cabo San Lucas Airport exists because Mexican authorities mistakenly built the runway there. The story I heard was that after construction was complete, they realized it was located in Cabo San Lucas, not San Jose del Cabo, where they intended to build a major international airport. At that time, Cabo San Lucas was just a sleepy fishing village, while San Jose del Cabo was already an established city.

Obviously, as Cabo became a hot tourist attraction, they

later decided to establish an international airport 40 miles west in Cabo San Lucas, named Los Cabos International. So, the 11,000-foot runway mistake was eventually justified. This runway, well paved, was just concrete with some shacks in a field of dried shrubs, but no one was there when I first started to use it. There was some fencing, a ramshackle building, and a dirt road leading to town. Often, there was the smell of bull crap, which we once smelled in the plane after takeoff!

Landing there saved the need for a 40-mile taxi drive out of the International Airport near San Jose Del Cabo down a long, single-lane highway. This road was notorious for accidents and deaths, proven by the many crosses and memorials along the roadside. The unattended Cabo San Lucas Airport was more convenient but had its downsides. With no staff present, I could not be sure my plane would be there when I returned; in fact, several disabled planes with bullet holes sat beside the runway. Since this airport was unmanned, there was no pay phone, and we had no phone of our own at the time, prior to mobile phones. To alert a taxi driver, pilots would fly over the city of Cabo San Lucas in circles, which usually drew one out to the airport. Unfortunately, this did not always work, and on several occasions, I started walking the eight miles toward the city. Usually, I managed to flag down a cab to take me back to the airport. Over time, a guard was stationed there to watch the planes, and for several dollars a day, I had a little more peace of mind. Eventually, the airport grew and expanded, and a proper terminal building was constructed. It was not fancy and certainly not designed for thousands of passengers, but with fuel available and customs services added, it became a very desirable entry point compared to Los Cabos Int'l in San Jose del Cabo. It now serves charter flights from mainland Mexico, but no international flights.

Going through customs at a big international airport is much more complicated, with thousands of people and many planes flying in from all over. Customs at my local Cabo airport was simple, once the field added a customs agent in its growing sophistication. I would fly my plane from Yuma Naval Air Base directly to Cabo as my first stop in Mexico and go through customs there. Upon landing, we were greeted with a red carpet, military guards, and a customs agent who handled all the required paperwork right there at the plane, without having to go from office to office for the right stamps on the right documents. The Comandante also prepared my flight plan before departure, so I was ready to take off for home. At the same time, the airport crew carried the luggage into and out of the terminal, and we were offered complimentary margaritas and beer.

During my travels, I appreciated not having to wait for my plane to be refueled, as it was typically prepared and brought to the terminal from its parking space on the scheduled departure date. However, given that this was a foreign country, unforeseen issues sometimes arose. On one occasion, I was informed, as we ended our week and were ready to depart, that the airport had depleted its aviation fuel supply, with the assurance that more would arrive the following day. Since my departure filing mandated I leave within an hour that was not acceptable. Like the previous missing gas cap incident, I requested that fuel be syphoned from another aircraft not scheduled for immediate use. Fortunately, they complied and drained fuel from another plane in buckets to fill my tanks. It was no small undertaking, as the C340 required about 160 gallons. This experience underscored the importance of ensuring the aircraft was refueled upon arrival.

Flying into Mexico, especially in the 1980s, had its drawbacks. Weather forecasts were limited, and air traffic controllers at major airports often operated with restricted or no radar capability, frequently requesting position updates. Before GPS, pilots provided estimated position reports based on visual land references or distant VOR radials. Instrument flying required reporting locations, as controllers routinely asked both general aviation and commercial pilots for their positions. I felt altitude data was considered more reliable than position estimates derived from landmarks, especially when flying IFR, to avoid collisions.

In one of the first trips to Mexico in 1984, I flew my Cessna 210 with our young daughter and baby son to the Hotel Cabo San Lucas airstrip. At the time, this was one of the major hotels in the area, though not directly in the town of Cabo San Lucas, but a few miles east up the coast of the gulf. By today's standards, it was minuscule. We were taking advantage of this hotel's strip to stay at another resort, the Twin Dolphins. My only information was its length and width, which should accommodate my small Cessna at the time.

As I circled and approached the strip, I felt confident it was in good enough shape to land. Just before touching down, my eye caught the wreckage of a small plane just off the side of the runway, a cause for concern. As my wheels touched down, I saw what appeared to be the end of the runway, far too short for my plane, in opposition to the information I had been given. I stood on the brakes, and as I reached the top of the little hill of the runway, I could see the rest of it, plenty of length. This was my first experience with domed, or arched, runways.

The Twin Dolphins was an architecturally modern hotel on the cliffside above the beach and blue waters of the Sea of Cortez. During our visit, a solar eclipse made the stark landscape and quiet atmosphere feel surreal. Though the hotel is gone, the cove remains popular with tourists and snorkelers for its clear water and diverse marine life.

Early in my Mexican flying career, a vacation took us down to Guaymas on the east side of the Gulf of Mexico, and we brought along our 80-year-old babysitter. It was a bit snug in our Seneca, a twin six-seater with 200-hp engines, but worth the help. For some reason, we got a later start than usual, and as we flew down the coast, the sun was lowering fast. Flying VFR (visual flight rules) prohibits flying at night in Mexico. I had heard stories of planes locked up after landing and owners paying heavy fines. I knew we would not make Guaymas in daylight, so out came the map, and the closest airport was Bahia Kino.

To my surprise, this turned out to be a joint civil and military airbase. Landing of a civilian aircraft. We landed just before sunset and were met by the comandante sporting a large gun. Fortunately, He was cordial when we asked about the availability of a cab. "Lo Siento," he said, and indicated there were no cabs at the airbase. Landing of civilian aircraft was legal, but very few ever did it; it was mostly military. There were no phones to call a cab. We asked how we could get to a hotel for the night. His only suggestion was to walk across the desert to town, the only place with hotels. We could see the lights of the town, about a mile away across a scrub desert.

He offered several of the military men to accompany us to the city limits. This was the only option, though not ideal since our 80-year-old babysitter had only bedroom slippers on. I asked why we needed the armed military escort, since we could clearly see the lights of the town, and it was a straight walk across the desert. The whole time, I wondered if we would be shot during the trip, and no one would hear it. The answer to my question about the escort was, "It is the rattlesnakes." That became evident when one of the soldiers pointed out a rattler as we crossed the runway. When we finally reached a paved street, the military men hailed a city policeman. I am not sure how he did it, but the soldier told us the officer would drive us to a hotel. We 5 crammed into the screened back seat of the police car as he drove us around to several hotels, all full. Eventually, we got the last room in this small fishing village in the heart of tourist fishing season. We 5 crammed into one room and, with little sleep, caught a cab the next morning to the base and flew out without a hassle or a bribe. Probably a first for this military base and another uniquely Mexican experience to add to my repertoire.

On another trip, we decided to check out Mazatlán. We took friends with their two girls, along with our two children, and a high school girl to babysit. I flew my Navajo Chieftain, a ten-passenger, twin-engine, non-pressurized plane. This aircraft could carry quite a load but wasn't very fast. We stayed in condos just outside of Guaymas, in what was pretty much an American enclave. The place was right by shallow water, ideal for small children.

Our babysitter's arrangement included pay and the freedom to explore Mexico after we returned from dinner, as long as she was back by 8 a.m. On departure day, she still hadn't returned by 10 am, delaying our departure and making us a nervous wreck. We were more than relieved that the story she fed us was that she fell asleep on the beach and did not wake up until morning, but with whom we will never know, or care. Just imagine if we had flown back to the US without her and had to explain why to her parents!

The following year, we returned to Guaymas with our kids and two young adult babysitters. We enjoyed these condos in Guaymas for being clean, close to the water, and affordable. After renting a car at the airport, guards stopped us as we drove up to the condo entrance. Seeing no reason for delay, I drove past them directly to our unit. We unpacked, changed into our bathing suits, and settled on the beach.

After all, it was a hot day in Mexico, and we were tired from traveling.

After about an hour, a gentleman dressed in a suit walked up to our little beach blanket and asked us to leave. Why? Everything looked fine. We had prepaid for the condo. He explained that he was from the American embassy, and the Mexican police were raiding and evicting many people from the condos. Apparently, squatters had taken over several of them when the owners were back in America. The problem had become so widespread that the Mexican authorities were going condo to condo, physically removing squatters, and they didn't want us around in case things turned nasty.

So we left for several hours but were able to return to the beach later. Our two very pretty babysitters quickly became the highlight for the young Mexican policemen. We have a great picture of the girls sporting the officers' guns tucked in their bikinis and arms around the officers.

The weather in Baja was usually clear with no clouds, summer or winter, though occasionally a storm would occur. The big problem, especially before 2000, was that weather reporting was difficult to obtain. Once, flying down Baja to Cabo San Lucas, about 150 miles before reaching the airport, I saw a black wall of clouds ahead. There are small strips down the peninsula, and with me was my trusty aviation map, always a must in the cockpit. Not far ahead, just before the rain, was Serenaded, a dirt strip not long, but a resort at the end of it.

Rather than turn around, this random strip was the answer for the moment, and with a hotel nearby, it was a place to sleep if the weather did not clear up. This hotel was one of many small outposts along the gulf, a resort for pilots. There were roads to it, but I don't think many tourists would drive down to these little, faraway, rustic getaways. Our kids enjoyed the beach right there, and we spent the night. The next day, the weather was CAVU, clear, and visibility was unlimited.

It was the unexpected weather on trips like this that made the rule: be sure to have gone through customs at the border.

Another episode with the weather happened while returning from Cabo San Lucas. The sky was clear as we took off, but about 100 miles north, the high clouds started to lower, scattered at first but building. The plan at that point was to land at Loreto, a fairly large airport by Baja standards. It had a tower and even IFR approaches. As the visibility closed in, I called the tower for an IFR clearance. I received it and tried to get the frequency of the VOR for the approach.

I wasn't the only plane trying to pick up the VOR's radial frequency. A Cessna 414 coming down from the north at 16,000 feet was also calling the tower about the VOR frequency. We were both within range to get at least a weak signal, but nada. The response from the tower was, "Sorry, it isn't unusual for the frequency to short out in rainy weather."

Fortunately, I was over water and didn't have to worry about mountains as I slowly descended around the clouds to find the airport. The Cessna, at a higher elevation, had to figure out a way down. That experience kept me from counting on flying IFR in Mexico.

My 35 years of flying in Mexico ranged from seat-of-your-pants to much more sophisticated. I have always found the personnel respectful, pleasant, and professional, especially since 2000. Once, I was asked for a bribe by a commandante at one of the airports, but that was solved easily after a bit of negotiation. Nothing like that has happened since. From what I understand now, there have been many changes, mostly for the better.

CHAPTER 9: CHARITY FLIGHTS

I was often asked through the years to donate a flight for two to a location I would pick for wide interest and easy accessibility. One of the flights I offered was bid on and won by a podiatrist and his wife. The day we set was crystal clear with smooth air and great visibility. It took a little encouragement to convince his wife to go, not so unusual once someone only used to 747s saw just how small the plane really was. Even so, the Cessna 210 was a bit bigger, faster, and better equipped than most private aircraft. But tell that to a novice!

My usual bay flight departed from San Jose Airport, followed the peninsula north over Stanford University, crossed the Golden Gate Bridge, circled Alcatraz, then turned south over Oakland before returning to San Jose. We usually flew around 2,000 feet. But as I rounded the Golden Gate that day, the weather began to change. The air remained calm, but visibility quickly deteriorated. A dark cloud seemed to hang directly ahead. Just then, air traffic control advised me that Oakland was burning. It was the devastating Oakland Hills Fire of 1991.

I returned safely to San Jose, but not before the dramatic view of that blaze convinced the wife she had been right all along: in small planes, you can never be entirely sure what's waiting ahead.

In the late 1990s, I frequently flew Angel Flights volunteer missions that carried patients with chronic illnesses to medical centers and university hospitals at no cost. Many families lived too far away to travel otherwise. Pilots covered all expenses themselves, but the reward was knowing someone reached vital care they might have missed. I crisscrossed the state, picking up patients and delivering them where specialists could see them.

Another effort I joined was the Mother's Milk Bank. A group of women donated breast milk for infants whose mothers could not produce enough on their own or who required special nourishment. I would pick up the collected milk at Santa Clara Valley Medical Center and fly it to San Bernardino, where a remarkable family fostered these infants. Their home was lined with cribs, each occupied by a newborn needing to be fed around the clock. Volunteers helped, but it was still a private house, not a clinic. Seeing the dedication of that family, who poured themselves into these children day and night, I couldn't help but think of them as true angels.

For many years, I also flew with the flying doctors, Los Médicos Voladores. This group traveled to small towns in Mexico and rural areas in the American Southwest with large underserved populations. Most of the volunteers were dentists, hygienists, and physicians who paid their own way and gave four or five days to provide care. The effort was no small undertaking: crates of equipment had to be flown in to transform a schoolroom or orphanage into a temporary clinic.

By the first day's end, the makeshift dental lounge chairs

were in place, suction units, lights, drills, and trays of instruments ready for use. Patients, children, and adults alike arrived from miles away, waiting in the hot sun for a turn. Extractions were common; at the end of the day, a bucket might be filled with teeth. But the medicos also performed root canals and more complex procedures, all in that improvised setting.

Local sponsors often hosted meals for the volunteers, a gesture of gratitude that balanced the long hours of work. A typical trip required four to six plane loads of volunteers, each flown in by doctors and dentists themselves, landing at small airports before being driven to the villages.

The poverty and lack of access to care in those communities were hard for most Americans to imagine. Yet the program was a true exchange: villagers received relief and treatment, while Los Médicos Voladores gained the deep satisfaction of using their skills where they were most needed.

On one of these flights in the spring of 2021, I had two dentists and a hygienist in my Cessna 340 heading to Thermal, not far from Palm Desert. This was the summer of the multiple fires in California. The sky was filled with smoke traveling hundreds of miles across the state. I was flying at 15,500 feet VFR with flight following above the smoke. The air was better at that altitude, and for a pressurized plane, a good altitude with no thermals. I was unable to see the ground at that altitude, but the visibility ahead was good.

As the smoke started to rise and my forward visibility was

deteriorating, I advised flight following that I was going up to 17,500. Again, the forward visibility was unlimited, and though thunderstorms were forecast, none were visible. After a while, listening to the radio, there were reports of deviations of planes due to these thunderstorms. I called Flight Following to ask about this activity, and just then, what seemed to be billowing clouds from under the smoke were rising all around me. I started to weave, not quite engulfed in the thunderstorm yet. This was the beginning of a possible disaster; thunderstorms are the great white sharks of the sky.

I advised flight control about the situation, asking for immediate clearance to 19,000 IFR to try to get over these darkening conditions, and which direction I should head. The dark clouds were billowing higher and higher. The controller suggested that I turn right, but just then, in doing so, we were engulfed in a thunderstorm. At that moment, it was like being eaten by a monster. This was an "Oh Shit" moment, actually an "Oh Shit, Oh Shit, Oh Shit" moment. This could have the makings of a total disaster.

It is hard to remain calm in a moment like that, but if not, I would not have been able to handle the situation. With heart racing and anticipating the worst, I had my hands full just keeping the airplane sunnyside up and not stalling, spinning, and plunging. I slowed the plane down to just above stall speed to reduce the forces on the wings. I lost all sense of directional control, and my altitude changes were over 10,000 feet per minute, due to the severe up and down drafts. The plane would turn on its axis by 120 degrees at one point and I felt I had almost lost it. A few more degrees and we would be upside down. If that happened, I would force the rotation and try to do a total roll. I have done rolls in a Navy jet, but I was not at the wheel, and it would be guesswork for me at that time. Lots of things to think about, but I really did not want to invert, which looked like a real possibility. A twin-engine is no jet.

To add insult to injury, Icing was developing on the wings, and the windshield was iced up as the hail pinged on the fuselage. I was busy turning on the deicing boots and pitot heat as well as the windshield alcohol. Air traffic control was telling me to head in a specific direction, but I could not hold a course. Coincidentally, my wife, who occasionally checks where I am using the FlightAware app, saw the blip on the screen indicating N340 going in tiny circles and assumed air controllers were really moving me all around the sky. She had no idea I was being bounced around by that thunderstorm.

Twenty minutes in a thunderstorm feels like hours. I was so thankful my three passengers remained quiet. Having a screaming and panicking passenger would add too much additional stress, and although I have a lot of confidence in my skills, it could have been fatal. They were not happy, but at least they were silent.

Finally, we were spit out of the thunderstorm and into a clear, calm sky, and I got complete control of the aircraft to land safely at Thermal. To say that was a huge sigh of relief is an understatement. Without a doubt, this was the closest near-death experience I have ever negotiated, and although I know I have a lot of confidence in my skills, I can't help but attribute some of it to Lady Luck once again.

After we landed in thermal, I called my mechanic and asked how one tells if there is structural damage to the plane. "Just check for wrinkles on the wings and body."

CHAPTER 10: EMERGENCIES AND RISKY FLYING

One might imagine that the previous story should be included in this chapter. Perhaps, but I'm dedicating this chapter to taking responsibility for the risks and decisions I made that perhaps were not the best. The thunderstorm certainly was the top of the list, but I feel that with the bad situation I was inadvertently dealt, I made the right decisions, used every skill in the book, and saved a nearly disastrous situation.

Another emergency occurred early on in my California flying days. My mechanic had advised me that the plane needed new rubber liners for the fuel tanks as part of routine maintenance. He recommended I first drain either one of the tanks dry before dropping it off, and so I set the date upon the return from an Idaho water rafting trip. My passenger, Art, remembers the trip vividly, and here are his memories:

It was about 40 years ago – we were about 45, maybe in the 1980s. Gordon and I went on an exciting Orange Torpedo trip in Idaho on the Salmon River. The trip there was just as exciting. Gordon flew us in his single-engine plane from San Jose Airport to Lewiston, Idaho. I'd only flown in a single-engine plane once before to go skiing with Gordon, so I was pretty inexperienced in a small plane.

When we took off from SJC, Gordon had oxygen placed in the plane's reserve tanks so he could fly higher and get us to our destination faster. We took off, we were soon wearing our oxygen masks, and when we were flying over Nevada, I noticed the oxygen gauge said "0". I told Gordon, and he said,

"The gauge is not correct and we will know when we are out of oxygen" -- (when we pass out???) -- When the oxygen bag doesn't inflate. Eventually, my O2 mask didn't inflate. I told Gordon my bag didn't inflate, and he dropped the plane down to 8000 feet, where you don't need O2.

By that time, we were flying over Utah, and the plane started to shake a bit. Gordon radioed to Lewiston, Idaho. They said we were approaching a thunderstorm, which was causing the plane to shake. When I heard the weather report, I was very concerned. Gordon chose to keep going through the inclement weather. Within about 15 minutes, it was raining and you could see lightning strikes on the ground.

All of a sudden, all of Gordon's instruments went out, which was caused by the electricity in the air. Luckily, Gordon is very intelligent and a good pilot. He radioed again to Lewiston, ID, that his instruments had gone out, and asked if they could pick us up on their radar. The controller in Lewiston said he did pick us up on his radar and gave Gordon a reading so he could use his compass to guide us to Lewiston. Very exciting, and I wondered if we were going to make it!! We could see the thunder clouds in a cylinder, and Gordon flew around the thunder cells. I found out later that if we got too near them, the plane could have been destroyed. Gordon told me to keep my eyes open for an area for an emergency landing if needed. However, we were in a very mountainous area! Lo and behold, we finally made it to Lewiston, ID, and I was very glad to be there – alive and well!!

The Orange Torpedo rafting trip was very exciting, fun, and peaceful compared to our flight! After a fun day of whitewater rafting out in the wilderness, and a great meal, the guides made a large teepee "sauna" with canvas over a large hole they dug. Then they shoveled hot volcanic rocks in the center of the hole, and poured cold water over the rocks to make it steam. About 8 or 10 of us sat around the edge of the hole, under the canvas, to enjoy our sauna. Afterwards, we all jumped in the river for a swim. We had fantastic river guides. I'd mentioned our exciting flight story to some of the members on the river trip who were professional airline pilots, and they were amazed at our story.

When the river trip was over, we bused back from the river to Lewiston, ID, where Gordon's plane was waiting for us. The Lewiston airport is very small, and we had the only plane there that I could see. Gordon said, "Let's go!" so we got in. And guess what?? The plane wouldn't start! I thought to myself, "Oh, good, I'm going to catch a commercial flight home!"

Gordon noticed a small hangar, about 100 yards from where our plane was parked. We walked over there, and Gordon met the airplane mechanic, who told us to pull our plane over to his hangar. We got the plane over to the hangar, and the mechanic removed the bonnet over the engine. He said, "The starter motor is no good," and that he could jump-start the plane to start it. He jump-started it and placed the bonnet back on the plane with the propeller going. Then Gordon said, "Jump in; we're going!".

We had plenty of gas to get home, but I was concerned that if the plane engine stopped, we would have a problem starting the engine again with no starter motor. I realized we could get a wind start to start the engine in the air if we had to.

It was a clear, beautiful day with no weather problems ahead. We were near Lake Tahoe, flying at about 9000 feet, and I noticed that one of the wing tanks was almost out of gas. I wondered if Gordon was going to completely drain the tank, which he'd told me needed to be serviced in San Jose, or if he would switch to the other wing tank before the engine stalled. Since we were close to the Sierras, I was concerned about stalling the engine. All of a sudden, I saw Gordon switch the wing tanks just before the engine stalled. I teased Gordon that he chickened out!!

We made it back to San Jose. It was a fun river trip, and our exciting flights made a great story!! I'm very glad you are an excellent pilot, Gordon!! And we're now in our 80s, still good friends, and still telling the story!!

Later that year, Judy and I planned to fly to Bend in the Cessna 210. As I was on a takeoff rollout out of San Jose, about to lift off the nose wheel, the engine quit. I was able to roll to a spot to exit the active runway, where I had to be towed to the FBO. The culprit was a fuel pump failure. At this point, I made a decision: it was time to get a twin-engine airplane.

I never really feared a loss of engine while flying over the countryside; I figured I could always find something flat to land on. But trying to land in a city was another matter. The frequency of my flights and the increasing likelihood of potential incidents convinced me it was time to begin twin-engine training.

On final approach to San Jose International in the Cessna 340

Another interesting event happened at San Jose International. Flying VFR from Southern California, I was on final down the ILS, though still on visual. I was cleared for RWY 30R, with the tower asking me to keep my speed up on approach. Five miles out, while descending, I was at 180 knots, roughly keeping up with what the commercial jets maintain. But to slow down to the proper approach speed of 100 knots, I first had to drop to 160 knots to lower the flaps the first 10 degrees, then down to 140 knots to lower the wheels and bring the flaps further down, planning to cross the threshold at 100 knots.

The C340 is a relatively fast plane and doesn't slow down quickly, especially while descending. I tried to keep the speed up since I was aware of a commercial jet behind me. Just as my wheels settled on the pavement, the tower shouted for me to immediately take the first right turnoff. The urgency in his voice made it clear that something was wrong.

I slammed on the brakes and nearly went up on two wheels, nose and right main as I veered onto the first turnout. I could almost feel the whoosh of the jet as it passed just off my tail. The tower's controller came back on the mic with a heavy sigh and said, "I'll never do that again." He had obviously misjudged the jet's closing speed, and we had just barely avoided a rear-end collision on the runway.

I have had several episodes of losing an engine, most in my twins, only once in the single Cessna 210 just before takeoff. In November 1987, while flying the Chieftain just after being requalified by the insurance company, I was just off the airport and making the usual left turn-out when I saw smoke from the port engine. Good thing it was the left engine, since I was already looking that direction.

Fires in an engine can cause real trouble, since the wing itself can burn and deform. It didn't take long to shut the engine down and get it back to the mechanic. I can't recall what exactly caused it.

Speaking About Fires. Coming back to San Jose in my 340, I caught a smell that just wasn't right. An electrical fire? At altitude over Nevada, with not many airports available, that's not the smell you want to notice.

I keep my fire extinguisher just behind the co-pilot's seat, and I reached for it. At the same time, I started shutting down most of the electrical equipment. I hated turning off the radios, but they were high on the list of probable offenders. The heater was off; that's the one thing that actually has a real fire in it, right in the nose of the plane. I always notice its smell when I turn it on, but usually once it starts running, it clears up.

All lights were off. No flames. The smell began to fade back toward normal. I checked outside: the engines weren't spewing fire. Decision time. I slowly powered the electrical equipment back on, waiting each time to see if the smell returned. I didn't bring everything back online, just the essentials, and I felt confident enough that the problem had passed. My mechanic checked it out later, and I never had a repeat. Maybe it really wasn't a fire, maybe just a sensitive nose, and a sensitive nose for trouble.

1987 wasn't a good year for problems.

Flying my Seneca out of Bend, Oregon, on an IFR departure, I was just entering the clouds when the right engine started surging. While it was happening, I recalled an article about a twin that went down when the pilot spent too much attention trying to manage a surging engine. He forgot the first rule of flying an airplane. Fiddling with the fuel levers, he lost control, spun, and crashed.

I didn't want to repeat his mistake. In the clouds, with no room for error, I kept it simple: a controlled shutdown of the engine. With one good engine, I flew the ILS into Redmond, just a few miles away, and got a mechanic to fix the problem. Fuel pumps are quick repairs.

In December 1993, flying to Eagle, Colorado, for a shoulder repair meeting and, of course, skiing, I was shedding oil from the port engine of the Seneca. I was cruising at 17,500 feet over mid-Utah, enjoying the westerly winds and on oxygen when it happened. I shut the engine down and began a gradual descent; the airplane couldn't hold that altitude on one engine.

Over Cedar City, I saw a good-sized airport below. If I landed, though, I knew I'd lose at least a day waiting for repairs, probably longer. That meant no meeting and no skiing. My decision was made: continue to Grand Junction, a large airport with excellent mechanics and still within driving distance of Vail, my original destination.

That's the advantage of a twin: you don't necessarily have to put down immediately. You have options. But the truth is, a Seneca can't climb very well on one engine, and I started to wonder if it had enough power to clear the smaller mountains between me and Grand Junction. Maybe not the most rational plan. If necessary, I could always follow the Colorado River through the valleys.

The airplane made it into Grand Junction, and we rented a car for the short drive to Vail. Over the next four days, we skied, including one unforgettable morning after a foot of fresh snow had fallen the night before.

In October, I lost electrical power in the Chieftain on a sunny day flying with a friend's son out of Concord, CA. Never fun to lose communication with the tower, especially flying around the San Francisco Bay area, where there are three huge commercial airports, San Francisco, Oakland, and San Jose, not to mention about half a dozen smaller ones. This is heavily controlled airspace, with everyone connected to the approach and departure controllers.

The book says to use the transponder code for lost communications, letting controllers know you have a problem. Way back in basic training, we were required to memorize the color code from the tower for landing without a radio. Flashing green meant continue approach. Green meant cleared to land. Red meant give way to other landing planes. Flashing red meant get out of there.

First, though, I had to get their attention without colliding with another aircraft or interfering with the approach patterns. I flew 1,000 feet over midfield and rocked my wings. It worked. I got my flashing green light. What a relief. I guess that's why color blindness is disqualifying for a pilot's license. I don't know how often this system is used, but for me, at least once.

The paint job after purchasing the Cessna 340 lasted about 18 years. I had it redone at the original painting contractor in Lincoln since the first job had held up so well, even with the plane not hangered. A friend flew me up in his homebuilt RV-6 so I could pick it up. At around 75, squeezing into his small aircraft was tough on my joints, but I certainly appreciated the ride. I have never assumed a plane is ready to fly just because it came out of a shop, and, in fact, things never seem to be the way I left them or like them to be!

After paying for the paint job, I did my usual preflight inspection. Thank goodness I did. I've never assumed a plane was ready to fly just because it came out of the shop, any shop. During my walk-around, I discovered someone had forgotten to connect the rudder to the cables. I'm not sure how the plane would have flown without rudder control, but I was glad I didn't have to find out. Of course, the paint shop blamed the repair shop for the oversight.

When an aircraft is flown frequently over many years, engines inevitably deteriorate. They become unreliable or reach the end of their service life, and the right time for replacement is determined by the mechanic's judgment. That time came in March 2018, when both engines had to be replaced. Along with the expense, there was also downtime with no flying. When the plane finally came back into service, I took the first flight on June 9, 2018, and went through the prescribed new engine break-in procedures over several days.

During that time, I began considering getting a partner on the plane. Costs were rising, not just fuel but taxes, insurance, and tie-down fees. At 76, the thought of slowing down was creeping up on me. I arranged to show the plane to two prospective partners.

The next day, we took off from San Jose for a demonstration flight. I flew left seat, one potential buyer was in the co-pilot's seat, and the other was in the back. We weren't far from San Jose, about to let the prospective pilot take the controls, when I looked left and saw oil spewing from the cowling. This wasn't a trickle but a steady flow. The instruments were still in range, but I shut down the port engine and advised air traffic.

Since my mechanic was at Reid-Hillview and he had just put in the new engines, I preferred to return there to save repair hassle. Both Reid-Hillview and San Jose were less than five miles away. Reid-Hillview had a 3,000-foot runway, while San Jose had an 11,000-foot runway. Runway length versus repair convenience. I chose Reid-Hillview.

It was another smooth landing, and I was even able to make the right-hand turns off the runway, up the ramp, and to the mechanic's area without a tow. In spite of the safe handling and demonstration of how well the aircraft performed on one engine, the two gentlemen weren't interested. Maybe my decision to take the shorter runway factored into their choice, rather than how well the plane handled.

Hanging up The Wheels

In May 2023, my daughter and her family drove to Sunriver

for a week, and I flew up to join them for a couple of days. Since Sunriver Airport was closed for runway repairs, we landed in Bend, about 30 miles north. A couple of days later, I taxied to the only self-fuel tanks on the field and pulled parallel to the pumps, positioning the left wing close enough to ensure the hose would reach both tanks. After refueling, I started to taxi out. At the end of the fuel shed, there was a small, paved road that looked like the exit ramp from the pumps, but with potentially damaging gravel adjacent to it. In my narrowed attention to keep on the road, not looking left, the tip of the wing caught a small post. The impact ignited a spark in the strobe light, and the wing, newly filled to the tip with fuel, went up in flames.

I yelled at Judy, "Get out," and she literally dived down the steps without her shoes or ID, and crawled under the plane to the far side. I immediately shut off the fuel and followed her through the back door and down the steps. We moved well away as the fire grew and others ran out of their hangers to witness what was happening. With 5,000 gallons of jet fuel and aviation gas nearby, the risk was potentially catastrophic, but fortunately, the tanks were thick and did not ignite. I stood by and, with a sinking heart, watched my plane being destroyed by flames. It turns out the field has no fire department on-site since it is an uncontrolled airport, and it took twenty minutes for Bend's crew to arrive. Later, I learned that the small, paved road I used was for refueling trucks, not for taxiing, and there had been no signage to indicate that.

This isn't how I pictured my last flight... Insurance for pilots

127

over 80 is almost impossible to maintain, and even before this incident, Avemco had notified me of increasing premium due to the over 80 age range. By the way, they were stellar in covering the cost of damages for the loss of the plane and damage to the fuel island.   A month later, I was diagnosed with cancer, adding to a very bad few months, and began chemotherapy and radiation, which would have prevented me from passing the medical requirements for my license in any case. After 50 incredible years of flying adventures, the time had finally come to hang up my wings.

Left wing clipped fuel station infighting from wing tip light

CHAPTER 11: THERE ARE OLD PILOTS AND BOLD PILOTS, BUT NO OLD, BOLD PILOTS.

That phrase is generally true. Many accidents have come from poor decisions or poor execution in the air. The incidents I have shared show some were the result of mechanical issues, some were weather-related, and some were the result of personal decisions, and yes, a lot of luck. Through it all, I was very lucky to enjoy fifty years of flying across this country and beyond.

Writing this brief history has been rewarding, giving me a chance to relive adventures and misadventures, and thankfully, I am still here to write about it. Even though readers couldn't actually go along for the ride, I hope you have enjoyed this vicarious escapade called aviation.

Gordon Levin, MD
glevinmd@gmail.com

Reflections from Fellow Travelers

Over the years, I've been fortunate to share the skies and the adventures of flying with many friends. A few of them have shared their own memories of those journeys.

Jason Balaban recalls

I had the opportunity to join Gordon on his annual flight adventure to Alaska. It was truly the most exciting thing I have ever done. I cooked dinner the first night after marinating filet mignon at home for two days in garlic, onions, and spices in a large baggie. I must say all seven of us devoured that delicious meal on the beach just before our kayaking expedition.

Gerry remembers

In 1990, Gordon and I flew to Alaska, rented an Archer, and off we went north from Anchorage to Whitehorse. Then we followed the railroad to Skagway until the last minute, when we realized trains go under tunnels at the last second, and we quickly made a 180-degree turn. We stopped at Dawson Creek as the Yukon ice was just breaking up, and then went to Inuvik. When we finally found it, the runway was underwater. Fortunately, the Canadian Air Force had a base, and they let us land to refuel. Almost got lost on the way to Fort Yukon; the compass and navigation aid were useless. Just followed the Yukon River.

Michael Gold shares

At Glacier Bay, we were dropped off at the Cove by ferry, unloaded kayaks, and set up tents. Judy immediately took over organizing our campsite and cooking dinner, steaks, and bourbon. The orcas arrived later for their evening meal and sang us to sleep with loud, rhythmic breathing as they cleared their blowholes. At daybreak, after awakening from a peaceful slumber, I was surprised to find myself alone during the night. The rest of our group had moved their tents forty yards away; evidently, my snoring was not as melodious. Not a single thank-you, but I still maintain it prevented an invasion from the nearby bear family.

Kayaking to the glacier and watching a calf, then hiking and spotting rather large wolf prints, was the next day's adventure. On our flight from Sitka to Ketchikan, the clouds rolled in as we approached the airport with zero visibility. Sitting beside you in the cockpit, I tried not to show fear, but as the flight controller radioed that he could not find us on the radar and with military jets using the same airspace, steep mountains on either side, you remained calm and dropped down below the white-out. We were dead center on the runway. I was very impressed and thankful.

ABOUT THE AUTHOR

Now retired after fifty years of orthopedic surgery and flying, Dr. Gordon L. Levin enjoys a quieter life of woodturning, golfing, and charitable work through the Rotary Club.

He began his aviation journey after earning his M.D. and joining the U.S. Navy as a Flight Surgeon, a role that included months of intensive training and combat flights in Vietnam. Over five decades, he logged more than 3,500 hours in the air and experienced the full spectrum of flying thrills and challenges.

www.ingramcontent.com/pod-product-compliance
Lightning Source LLC
LaVergne TN
LVHW051244080426
835513LV00016B/1723